EVOLVENZA®

The Evolution of Consciousness

Reincarnation

VITALIANO BILOTTA

THOUGHTS OF THE GREATS

commented on in the light of the teaching of the Masters

GENERAL DISCOURSE ON WISDOM

An interactive narrative

Translated from the original Italian edition

First Italian edition October 2011
First reprint October 2012
ISBN 978-88-904788-2-6

First English Edition July 2015
ISBN 978-1-908421-14-2

Published by
Saturday Night Press Publications
England.
snppbooks@gmail.com
www.snppbooks.com

Printed by Lightning Source
www.lightningsource.com

www.snppbooks.com

© *Cover design by Ann Harrison - Saturday Night Press Publications*
Background design © newyear at www.shutterstock.com

TABLE OF CONTENTS

EVOLVENZA®

Many years ago a group of friends came together to read and comment on the teaching that came to them from the expanded consciousness, which we call Guides or Masters. This consciousness manifests itself through great Italian and foreign mediums and reiterates that the ultimate goal of the evolutionary period called man is the evolution of the consciousness. They therefore called this gathering of friends "evolvenza", which is the synthesis of the Italian phrase "evoluzione della coscienza".

Over time Evolvenza (www.evolvenza.it) became an aggregation point for some mediums who not only read the teachings with the friends but were themselves a channel for other teachings. Later, they began to apply the Guides' teaching to the life of each of them, working in this way on narrative frameworks that answered the question, "Why is life like this?" For they believe that a story is an indispensable means to transmit a method of applying the Guides' teaching to life.

PREFACE

The phrase 'General Discourse on Wisdom' is used by the Spirit Guides who manifest themselves through great mediums to indicate the vast body of truths that initiates of all times and all religions have communicated throughout history.

For instance, the concept immortalized in the maxim "Do unto others as you would have them do unto you" is a rule that, contrary to popular belief, has a great many precedents.

Let us look at some of them, including that of the founder of Christianity.

Buddhism: *A state that is not pleasant or delightful for me must be so for him also; and a state which is not pleasant or delightful for me, how could I inflict that on another?* (Samyutta Nikaya V 353.35-354.2).

Confucius: (551-489 BC): *What you do not wish for yourself, do not do to others* (Analects 15, 23).

Jesus of Nazareth: *Always treat others as you would like them to treat you* (Matthew 7:12; Luke 6:31).

Jainism: *A man should wander about treating all creatures as he himself would be treated* (Sutrakritanga 1.11.33).

Islam: *Not one of you is a believer until he desires for his brother that which he desires for himself* (40 Hadith of an-Nawawi 13).

Rabbi Hillel (60 BC – 10 AD): *What is hateful to you, do not to your fellow men* (Shabbat 31a).

The concept expressed in these statements, which is the expression of the highest human wisdom, is an integral part of the 'General Discourse on Wisdom', a term extended in this book to everything said by the Great thinkers and philosophers in all ages, here set into the framework of the Guides' teachings.

I received the teachings laid out in this book over the span of almost fifty years through mediums that I knew personally, all over Italy. These sources were or are called *Cerchio Medianico Kappa, Chesed, NAF, Umanità e Movimento, Cerchio Marina, Soggetto, Il Silenzio delle Stelle, Exodus, Onda G, Cerchio Firenze 77, Cerchio Ifior, Pietro Ubaldi, and Entità A.*

I also became familiar with these teachings by reading foreign sources such as Allan Kardec, Kryon, Ramtha, Jane Roberts, Eva Pierrakos, and others. The episodes narrated in the book, which take place in and around Rome, provide helpful suggestions for applying the teachings to daily life.

Vitaliano Bilotta

DOUBT

"The superhighway seems like an expanse of asphalt that has nothing to do with us," said Roberta.

They were travelling through a valley thick with ilex trees, where the rhythm of the car engine provided a subtext to their thoughts. Julius looked at the vegetation which every so often broke into the expanse of asphalt. Roberta's hand followed the course imposed on her by the steering wheel. They spoke only if their thoughts demanded words. As sales representatives for dry-cleaning and laundry equipment they travelled together for work.

Roberta was forty years old and had always loved human wisdom. Julius was sixty and had always loved superhuman wisdom. Roberta studied the thoughts of the Greats of all time; Julius studied the thoughts of the Guides who manifest themselves through great mediums and applied them to his own life and that of others.

Roberta was the first to break the silence "According to your Guides, how can **Descartes**' statement – *Dubium sapientiae initium*, be interpreted? It means Doubt is the beginning of knowledge and affirms the importance of systematic doubt, summing up the Cartesian method."

They were driving along a long straight stretch that disappeared into the darkness of a tunnel. Julius shifted in his seat and in turn fired back another question "Does doubt pertain to the mind or to consciousness?"

"It pertains to being," Roberta answered.

"What part of being?"

Roberta did not answer.

"See", Julius said, "human wisdom does not answer these questions because if it knew the answer, it would not be human any more. Doubt pertains to the world of the mind, not that of consciousness, where the duality of I and not-I no longer exists. Thus doubt ceases to exist."

"Why is doubt not part of being?" Roberta asked.

"It is part of the developmental period called man, and this is understandable – if we accept the existence of other planes of existence, where life continues beyond what the evolutive average of incarnate beings considers the only life possible."

They approached a service area and Roberta slowed down to fill up the car. They went into the snack bar and ordered two coffees. They sipped slowly, talking about doubt. Once they were back in the car, Roberta remarked "It's true, coffee has to be as hot as the inferno, black as the devil, pure as an angel and sweet as love."

"Who said that?" Julius asked.

"**Talleyrand**."

"It is an astral truth of his," Julius commented.

"What does that mean?"

"Someone who can meditate so much on coffee feels that drinking it is an important sensation, and sensation is an activity of the astral body of the individual. That is why I said 'astral truth'."

"What is the 'astral body'?" Roberta asked.

"It is the body that makes it possible for the physical body, the one in which we now have our awareness, to have sensations, emotions, and desires."

"Meanwhile, what is the physical body?"

"It is the aspect of the individual that manifests itself on the plane of physical matter. The individual's lower bodies, as the Guides call them, are the physical, astral, and mental bodies. They change with every incarnation and are suited to the degree of evolution attained by the individual in the course of his past lives."

"I'm missing the 'mental body'," said Roberta.

"The 'mental body' gives the physical body the ability to think.

"The physical, astral, and mental bodies all together give shape – one could say – to the individual's I: in other words to his or her way of existing while still a human being."

As the car gobbled up the miles, something Roberta had read about cars popped into her mind. The line, whose author she did not remember, was: "Men put as much self-love into their cars as they do gasoline."

She asked Julius why, in his opinion, that line had come to mind.

"Maybe you intuited that a lot of I is hidden in a car," Julius said.

"How can one's I be hidden in a car?" Roberta asked.

"First let's see how the Guides explain the I", Julius said, "and then how it can hide in a car. The I is the principle of awareness contained in the world of phenomena, in 'duality', thus it is subject to separateness. But as such, the I does not exist; it is only a necessary illusion for an individual so that he or she can evolve. Why an illusion? Because the I is egoism and egoism is an illusion: an unreality, even if, as human beings, we are a product of the I. Our physical matter exists because the I exists: it is the 'code or mental ovum' which creates on the physical plane a body suited to expressing that I. This process is promoted – is Guided by the consciousness, but it is the I that creates us as human beings; our physical matter exists because the I exists."

"What is the 'mental code'?" Roberta asked, randomly choosing one of the things she had not understood.

"First let's see what the 'code' is and then we shall see what the 'mental code' is," said Julius. Meanwhile, he was thinking how far the teaching of the Guides had to travel to be accepted and how much more distance it had to cover to be understood. Even Roberta, who had made human wisdom her life passion, had a hard time managing to accept the existence of a higher wisdom.

"The code is a scheme", Julius went on, "a line of tendency of the various sublevels, which has to do with vibrations. In a fixed time called T which is the 'unit of change' – a time that the Guides fix as constant, – every individual emits vibrations on the various sublevels; these vary from one sublevel to another and one individual to another."

"Can you give an example?" Roberta asked.

"Certainly. Right now we are travelling through a tunnel and both you and I, like everyone else in every moment of their lives, have emotions, thoughts, and sensations. For example, as soon as we entered the tunnel, I was afraid because I found myself suddenly immersed in the dark and I couldn't see anything anymore. I thought it was better for you to slow down, which you did not do, etc. Well, this instant of my life, first the fear and then what I thought, were at that moment the 'vibratory rules' of my being. In particular, the fear was a vibration of my 'astral body' and what I thought was a vibration of my 'mental body'. These 'vibratory modes', which vary from one individual to another, are called 'codes' by the Guides."

"So the codes express our entire life," Roberta commented.

"Exactly. There is not one instant of our life that is not a vibration and thus a code, thus a mathematical expression, and thus perfect justice. Now let's move on to the mental code," Julius said. "The 'mental code or ovum' is given by the sum of the 'thought forms' produced by an individual in the course of his or her life – and also by some thought forms produced in earlier lives. Thought forms manifest themselves as 'causes' in the life that the individual lives. Therefore, the 'mental code is a product of the I; it is the I's most perfect creation and is what limits us because it is the I's reverberation on the mental plane."

"Where is my I hiding at this moment?" Roberta asked.

"Everywhere. If this car did not belong to the company we work for but was yours, it could hide in your possession of the car because for you the car could be a status symbol. Or it could be hidden in your driving. While driving, the I of many people feels protected by the car body and becomes aggressive towards other drivers or, as often happens, towards those who are less expert drivers.

"The I completely controls life in the developmental period called man; indeed, man is such, precisely because he is dominated by the I. In fact, when man transcends the I, he ceases being man."

They came to a sharp curve and Roberta slammed on the brakes. In front of them stretched a long row of idling cars. She turned on the hazard lights and slowly fell into line.

Roberta said, "An accident must have just happened because there is all the commotion of the first responders."

A little later the cars began slowly to thin out. They glimpsed the joyless blinking of an ambulance light. A semi-destroyed car blocked the road and another one was a smoking carcass.

"I don't remember where I read, I think in an English dictionary of ideas, this definition of accident," Roberta said as they came alongside a sheet covering a body. "An accident is a situation when presence of mind is useful, but absence of body is even more useful."

"Under that sheet is a creature who has just left his physical body behind", Julius commented, "so have some respect."

"That is, he died," Roberta simplified.

"He passed on. He moved his awareness from the physical plane to the astral plane that is to say he abandoned the physical plane; because of the wounds caused by the accident, he put aside his physical body."

"So now where does he live?"

"Like I said, in the astral body, just as earlier he lived in the physical body. Could you tell me again that definition of accident?" Julius said.

"An accident is a situation when presence of mind is useful, but absence of body even more useful," Roberta repeated. They passed the accident site and resumed their normal speed.

"You see", said Julius, "this saying too – the fruit of human intelligence – is completely mistaken from the standpoint of the Guides' teachings; even though it does have a subtle humour."

"Why?" asked Roberta.

"Because talking about 'presence of mind' and 'absence of body' is completely illusory. Even if our spiritual culture believes that on one side the mind exists and on the other matter, in other words, the body, the reality is that mind and matter are one and the same."

"There's no difference between them?"

"No, because 'physical matter', that is to say, the physical body, is the reflection of energy, that is to say, the astral body. The astral body is the reflection of idea, in other words, of the 'mental body', and the mental body is the reflection of the 'akashic body', that is to say of consciousness because the All is in Everything. Thinking that man can have an experience only with the physical body and not with all the other bodies means not having intuited the true nature of the developmental period called man."

Meanwhile, Roberta had become distracted and missed the right exit from the superhighway. She went on to the next exit and took advantage of the mishap to remember another line by the English philosopher **George Moore**: "The wrong road always seems the most reasonable."

"What do you think of that?" she asked.

"That for the Guides, no road is wrong", Julius answered, "because choosing a road, even if it is the wrong one, justifies that choice."

"I don't understand…"

"In Reality there is nothing to understand, but to comprehend," Julius said. "If a person makes a mistake of any kind, it is because he needed that mistake. Thus, in the general economy of the development of that individual, it was not an error but a necessary act on the path to comprehension."

Now they were traveling fast while Roberta searched her memory for the thought of a great man that could not be corrected by the teaching of the Guides. A thought by **Socrates** came into her mind, reported by **Plato**, concerning fame. Roberta wanted to reduce Julius to silence in front of a truly major thought and said "Fame is the perfume of noble actions. What would your Guides have to say about these words?" she asked.

"To answer you, I would have to understand the true meaning," Julius answered.

"I believe the line means that fame is the just recognition of noble actions," Roberta offered.

"If the line means that, the Guides would say that within the Law, there do not exist noble or ignoble actions but only actions and what they determine or could determine in the inner life of the individual."

"Then quality action does not exist?" said Roberta.

"The quality of an action is given by the quality of the intent with which the individual performs that action. Because behind every action there is an intent that determines it, and this is the true value of an individual."

"In your opinion was Plato a great man?" asked Roberta, to change the subject.

"The Guides have said more than once that Plato was a medium – an instrument, a means, a channel as we say now – and that in his writings he reported the wisdom that was communicated to him during his trances. Plato is a Great of the General Discourse on Wisdom."

"You have talked about this other times, but in reality what is this 'discourse'?"

"I have only mentioned it in passing because I was waiting for you to be interested in the Guides, whose teachings are an integral part of the General Discourse on Wisdom. The Teachings encompass all the works in which the great spirits of the past have handed down the wisdom that *from the beginning* has always been handed down to mankind. It is easy to intuit that the General Discourse on Wisdom has very little in common with what the religious organizations have built up around the Truth – both in terms of interpretation of the texts and of the relationship between the adepts, the faithful, and the conclusions that follow from this interpretation. In fact, the General Discourse on Wisdom knows no time, place or chosen people – and is impersonal – because the law of evolution is impersonal."

Roberta had exited the superhighway and stopped at the toll booth. She inserted her ticket to pay the toll while she rummaged around in her memory to dig up the thought of another great who might make things difficult for the teaching of the Guides.

She thought of a tercet from **Dante**'s *Purgatory*:

> *To run o'er better waters hoists its sail*
> *The little vessel of my genius now,*
> *That leaves behind itself a sea so cruel…*

"This is a metaphor that refers to the passage from hell to purgatory," said Roberta. "Hell is the 'sea so cruel' and purgatory the 'better waters'. How would your Guides explain this tercet?"

"First of all by denying the objective existence of hell and purgatory," Julius said. "For the Guides, hell is only a state of consciousness, which is by no means definitive. Purgatory is another state of consciousness – it too not definitive – and paradise is the state of consciousness called 'identification with God'; this one really is definitive, because it is the endpoint of the evolution of 'individuality'."

"What do your Guides say about the greatness of Dante?" Roberta insisted. "Is it possible that just one man was able to write all those lines that make up such a mighty monument of poetry?"

"In fact, the Guides say that the *Divine Comedy* was written as a form of clairvoyance; this means that Dante really saw the things he was describing on the various planes of existence.

"Nonetheless, what Dante was perceiving was, especially for the denser planes, what the beings of whom he was speaking had created around them. This is why he gave a much more genuine report of hell and purgatory than of paradise, where the beings whose thoughts he was recording could not go. The thoughts of the beings which Dante translated into verse, by means of his own Guide-entity are real; they are insights which come from the mental plane, the astral plane, and to a very small degree also from the akashic plane, that is to say, the plane of consciousness. However, it is true that it is not humanly possible to write, and in such a short time, these thousands of lines."

"How long did Dante take to write the *Divine Comedy*?"

"Contrary to what some of his biographers believe, Dante wrote the *Divine Comedy* in a little less than three years. However, he did not publish it all at the same time, but bit by bit, here too following the advice of his Guide-entity, who really was Virgil. Concerning the esoteric conclusions he reached, Dante knew many of the truths which the Guides later divulged, but not because he was a follower of some sect, or esoteric school. Dante was a very solitary person and had reached those all by himself, without any outside help, through his love for a creature, the famous Beatrice. By the way that was not her name; Dante called her Beatrice in his published works so that she, as an incarnate person, would not know about his love. There was little more than a formal relationship between Dante and Beatrice on the physical plane, but Dante did not experience it like this – quite the opposite: this love brought him very close to the point of abandoning the cycle of reincarnation.

"When the Guides speak of love for a being – like that between man and God – and say that one sole being can arouse in us a great feeling, they are referring to a cool love, devoid of passion, which has been useful to someone as a way. For Dante, this was the case. Furthermore, he never had carnal relations with Beatrice, but only little more than formal ones; in truth, there was never even a friendship between them. But all this did not concern him at all because what Dante wanted was not to be loved back but only to love –'to praise his lady' – as he wrote in *La Vita Nuova*. This should be read by anyone who wants to draw near to the teaching of the Guides because their wish for everyone is that a 'new life' should arise from love for one sole being and that, little by little, this may expand and become the cosmic love which Dante reached at the end of his spiritual journey. It is no coincidence that Beatrice accompanies him to the gates of the empyrean where God dwells: Dante reached God through Beatrice."

In the meantime, they were approaching the town of Belcastro, where they were supposed to call on some customers. The road twisted and turned along the curves of a hill in bloom.

"Can love for just one person do all this?" Roberta asked, being careful not to invade the opposite lane.

"All this – a superhuman love for just one creature can bring us into contact with the state of consciousness called God because every creature is in God."

"You said that love for Beatrice brought Dante very close to the abandonment of the cycle of rebirth. How close did it bring him?" Roberta asked.

"After having been Dante, the sentient being that was also Dante was incarnated only one more time, on a mission."

"What difference is there between leaving behind the wheel of birth and death and being incarnated on a mission?"

"Leaving behind the wheel of rebirth means not having to be incarnated anymore for the purpose of evolution. This happens when the individual has understood that the purpose of multiple incarnations is *learning to love*. At that point, the individual has overcome the evolutive period called man and begins to frequent the period of 'superman' which is not 'a man who is worth two', but *an individual who is no longer 'man'*. After this stage, the individual is getting ready to be the Law that has governed him up to that point."

"And when does the individual become incarnated 'for a mission'?" Roberta asked.

"Precisely then: when he no longer needs to be incarnated for evolution. The individual is incarnated for evolution until he understands that others are him himself. Afterwards, he is incarnated for a mission, that is to say, in order to help others understand what he has understood, that which he is already."

"What was the incarnation that Dante underwent for a mission?"

"In India in the eighteenth century. That time Dante was incarnated as a guru. By the way, you may be interested to know that **Paramahansa Yogananda**, another evolved being who helped spread Eastern wisdom in America, will be incarnated again for a mission. The Guides say that this event will take place after 2300. But let's get back to Dante. We have said that he, through Beatrice, who incidentally as a creature was not particularly evolved, found the state of consciousness that is God. It does not matter who Beatrice really was, or her state of evolution, because one who loves does not pose these questions, unless he loves for some end, and Dante's end was only the love that leads one out of subjective reality."

"Are you talking about love for an idealized woman?"

"No, the Guides mean love for another individual, that's all. The love that for Dante came through, or in, the form of a woman, between him and the state of consciousness called God."

"But why precisely that woman?"

"Because between them, a time existed from earlier lives, even if Beatrice became aware of this time only after she passed on. Then she found out, by intuition, about Dante's feelings. When she was alive, Beatrice would not have understood, and Dante kept his feelings hidden so as not to disturb her and because he was not interested in making it known. His desire was only love, as he writes in *La Vita Nuova*.

"Dante had reached the state of consciousness called love for the All, through love for this creature, who thus became the symbol for the totality of the All: in Beatrice was the All. Dante loved her with a love that involved in itself 'the All' and that, in order to be experienced, caused this woman to exist. But this love was independent of what that woman was in the 'physical photo-frames', and not only physical but also astral and mental. Theirs was a relation of consciousness and not a 'broad' relationship."

"Is what the biographers say true, that Beatrice has been historically identified as Bice Portinari?"

"No, it wasn't she. Beatrice's real name was totally different, but the Guides state that both Beatrice and Dante knew Bice Portinari."

"What benefit did Beatrice gain from being loved so much by Dante?"

"After she had passed on, Beatrice was drawn towards Dante, and from the higher planes of existence she helped him write the *Divine Comedy*. It is true that Beatrice passed on before Dante did; everything Dante recounts is true. It is true that Beatrice was a being that, through understanding the love Dante had for her, reached certain states of consciousness; however, this is a brainwave that came later."

"Did Beatrice, too, leave behind the wheel of births and deaths?"

"Some Guides have said that Beatrice was reincarnated many more times and that she has not yet finished the wheel."

"If Beatrice had been aware of this love before she died, would things have gone differently?"

"As an incarnate being she would not have understood. Their relationship was what it had to be. Dante lived only for a greeting from her, for her consideration of him. The mere fact that she said hello to him gave him the possibility to find his own beatitude."

"Therefore Dante loved Beatrice as an image?"

"He loved her as a transfigured meaning. These are states of consciousness still very far off for us, or at least for me. The Guides repeat that when we reach certain evolutive milestones we will realize, but already now we can intuit the greatness of a feeling that can go so far."

"So it is necessary to give an 'image' to one's love in order to then go beyond it?"

"Certainly, the image of Beatrice was a means but not the end for Dante; nonetheless, for him that means was necessary. Beatrice knew that Dante had a great reverence for her, that he considered her a 'gentle lady', as they said then, but would never have been able to understand the feeling he had about her. Even though Beatrice was a cultivated person, ready for the *stil novo*, for what Guinizelli, Cavalcanti, and Cino da Pistoia thought. Dante was helped greatly by Cino da Pistoia, even if Cino was not as evolved as Dante. At the beginning of his experience, Cino urged him to continue to love and not to fight this feeling, but rather to sublimate it; he was helpful to him in this sense."

"Your Guides have said that Beatrice was not particularly evolved; how could she have taken on all this spiritual importance for Dante?"

"Beatrice could have been a creature with a very low degree of evolution because for Dante that love was only an inner state of his own."

"Did Beatrice belong to a noble or a commoner class?"

"She belonged to a fairly well-to-do family: nobility that was falling into decay, but still influential. The Guides have explained that right before Beatrice passed on, she and Dante talked to each other and had some slightly less formal encounters – which for Dante were confirmations, imprimaturs, which gave him the strength, after Beatrice passed on, to transfigure this feeling even more and to bring him definitively close to his insight, which consisted in being 'love itself'. Nonetheless there was no real relationship between them, and Dante hid this great feeling from Beatrice, certainly not out of cowardice, but because he knew that she would not have understood and also this was not his purpose. In any case, no purpose existed because Dante's purpose was just that: love itself."

"What do your Guides say about Dante as a 'fugitive Ghibelline[1]'? Did he necessarily have to take up arms or could he have chosen differently?"

"Dante, at that moment, could not do otherwise; however, he abstained from killing. He took up arms, but when it came to killing someone, he avoided it because he had gone completely beyond that experience."

"It seems that Dante's personality was characterized by great pride. Was this self-respect or something else?"

"It was awareness that inside him there was something that few people had found. It was not pride but was the joy of someone who has found glory in himself through Beatrice, through what he calls 'the hope of the blessed'."

"Who was Dante's earthly teacher?"

"The Guides say Guido Guinizelli, the poetic influence of the *dolce stil novo* and Aristotelian atomist philosophy: Aristotle and Thomas Aquinas as instruments of knowledge, Guinizelli as a literary tool, and Cino da Pistoia as companion and friend, but only in the beginning. In his achievements, Dante was usually alone; he had a very lonely life. He really married Gemma Donati, but he never found with her the bond he felt with Beatrice because what existed between Dante and Beatrice transcended the world. In the world, Dante could have ties with anyone, but Beatrice represented God; she was

---

1. A member of an aristocratic political party in medieval Italy supporting the authority of the German emperors.

the bridge between man and Consciousness. Dante married Gemma Donati and lived for a period of time with her, but then she separated from him because she was not capable of understanding and left Dante to his meditations. But he had already found the state of consciousness *par excellence*."

"How did Dante meditate in his daily life?"

"He had a house, and in particular, a room in the house, where he would shut himself away for hours and hours, for entire days. His was a very conscious, very lucid meditation, and he wrote during this meditation, he wrote a lot. Dante wrote much more than has come down to us – a great deal more. The Guides say that he meditated so much on his feeling for Beatrice that, when he reached the Reality, he was silent; he never spoke again of this love because he had found that the only word was silence and that all his writings could have a meaning for some creature, just as they had had for him, but in the state of consciousness that he was discovering, they no longer had any value."

"Has the *Divine Comedy* come down to us in its complete state?"

"We have the whole corpus, but there are inaccuracies in many parts of it: missing lines, lines that were added. This is due to the many manuscripts and many commentators, who wrote over the text and not next to it, and sometimes it was not clear what was text and what was commentary. Thus there are comments inserted into the text, and in some lines there are Dante's words and the words of the commentary. In philological terms, we say that there are palimpsests. While with Petrarch we have his own handwriting and everything he wrote, with Dante this is not the case. His work has not been transmitted to us directly."

"Besides the *Divine Comedy*, are there other writings of the same value transmitted by clairvoyance?"

"Equal to it, no; the *Divine Comedy* was the supreme goal, which however Dante did not experience as a goal. The Guides explain that it was the goal, but not because he experienced it as such. In fact, evolution must not be sought: evolution is discovered.

"The Guides have also said that parts of *The Betrothed* were received through clairvoyance."

"Was **Alessandro Manzoni** also a medium?" Roberta marvelled.

"He was not an embodied instrument but was a very tormented psychic. His narration of the plague was inspired through a state of consciousness that now we could call 'ultraphanic'."

"And **Shakespeare**, was he a medium too?"

"No. The Guides explain that when Shakespeare wrote his works he was close to his final incarnation, but he had not yet reached the state of consciousness that is akashic beatitude, that is to say, Beatrice, to go back to the example of Dante."

"Speaking of Shakespeare, what would your Guides say about this beautiful line from Act I of *Hamlet,* in which Ophelia's father Polonius says to his other child, Laertes, who is about to leave for France – 'Those friends thou hast, and their adoption tried, grapple them to thy soul with hoops of steel'."

"What does that mean?" Julius asked.

"The friends you have, and whose friendship you have tested, fasten them to your soul with steel bands," Roberta paraphrased.

"You said a 'beautiful line' and it is unquestionably that", said Julius, "but we do not know all the equally beautiful lines said by countless unknown authors. We probably call this line beautiful because Shakespeare wrote it; here too reigns the absolute relativity of which the Guides speak. Concerning the first part of the line, it can be said that the Guides do not consider it important that a friendship be tested – because in Reality what counts is being a friend, without worrying about whether or not the others return your friendship."

"You mean we have to be indifferent?"

"On the contrary, we have to use the social relationship called 'friendship' to love, and if we truly love, we love disinterestedly, without expecting friendship from the person with whom we are friends. About the second part of the line – 'grapple them to thy soul with hoops of steel,' the comment is implicit in what I already said: if I am truly a friend, I do not need any test of friendship and thus I do not need to select anyone, not my friends nor the people who have proven to me that they are not friends."

"This is total indifference!" Roberta reacted.

"Not indifference but 'absence of passionateness' which is something different. If we have understood that we are our friend and also our enemy, we cannot help accepting both of them, without choosing between them, without being 'passionate'."

Meanwhile, they had reached the city and were moving slowly forward in heavy traffic, but very soon they decided to stop again for coffee. They entered a luxurious coffee shop. Fine pastries were on display, fine people were absent-mindedly drinking coffee at the counter. Roberta summed up the environment and said "*Il y a des gens qui rassemblent aux chansonnettes, qu'on ne chante qu'un certain temps.*" Then she walked towards the cash register.

"Who said that?" Julius asked.

"**La Rochefoucauld** – 'There are people who are like pop songs: they are sung for only one season'."

"What meaning do you give to this line?" Julius asked.

"I think it refers to worldly people who shine for one season and then, once their ambition has run its course, are boring and bored."

Sipping his coffee, Julius said "In many lines written by the greats there is often a vein of pessimism. Also for La Rochefoucauld, it seems that some existences have no purpose. For the Guides, instead, every existence, even the most ruinous, maintains its value intact, inherent in the experience of failure. This is why everyone is right just as they are."

"What do you say about the phrase – 'are sung for just one season'?" Roberta asked.

"I say that every experience is valid just one time. Even if it seems that it is repeated *ad infinitum*, it is never the same experience because the degree of evolution, the 'codes' and 'monads', the entire individual, the entire 'microcosm', the entire 'being' that lives that experience, is never the same as it was before."

Roberta laid the cup on the counter and let out a sigh "If this is reality, I will never manage to understand it!" she said.

"You will never manage to understand it in your current state of consciousness," Julius said. "When you gain access to a broader state of consciousness you will understand it, and do you know why? Because then you will be 'the portion of reality' that right now you are not."

They left the coffee shop and got back in the car. They had to call on an important customer, to whom they were supposed to sell two dry-cleaning machines, and they immersed themselves once again in the 'illusion' which Julius called everyday life, as is commonly meant by the term.

And yet the teaching of the Guides, which he studied so lovingly, did not allow him to live this illusion well because Julius *was not yet* the teaching. The Guides reiterate that the Law of an individual provides for his approach to the teaching when he is ready to understand it, but is still far away from 'being the teaching'. Many evolved religious and laypeople are completely unaware of the spiritual truths, precisely because, 'being already evolved', they have no need to know them.

Roberta, too, was beginning to intuit that life as commonly understood was an illusion, but she was still far away from assigning a transcendent purpose to this transitoriness. It was no coincidence that she had adopted as her own the saying by **Marcus Aurelius** – "Take without illusions, leave without difficulty," which expressed an important Stoic precept that man should not be attached to anything and must be ready to leave everything.

Julius had commented "At our level of evolution everything is an illusion. Nevertheless *it is an illusion that evolves*, and 'leave without difficulty' does not mean that what we leave has no purpose, but on the contrary that we leave it precisely because it has already given us its 'evolutive essence'."

A RACE THAT EVOLVES

Roberta and Julius were unusual sales representatives; they talked about topics that had nothing to do with their work. When they went to their company headquarters to be updated on the new models of machines, the director of sales would see them talking to each other with their technical papers in their hands, and would often comment to the other directors on the professionalism of those two reps. But Roberta and Julius were talking about their real interests: Roberta about human wisdom and Julius about superhuman wisdom.

During a meeting examining the characteristics of a new washing machine, Roberta whispered in Julius's ear – "I agree with **Henry Ford** when he says that 'the trouble with these modern conveniences is that they are so inconvenient'." She waited for Julius's comment, which was not long in coming "Progress, in the end, always wins out, and so it is never inconvenient. If something happens, it is always – and in any instance – for the best. The characteristic of the race to which we belong is precisely that we can use very advanced technology."

"Race?" Roberta said, not understanding.

"Yes, by 'race' the Guides do not mean white, black, yellow, etc., but a *soul group* which encompasses all the individuals who have in common the same evolutive needs, and thus are living analogous experiences…"

"Then 'race' according to your Guides, is the human race to which we belong?"

"That's exactly right!" Julius exclaimed, surprised at his colleague's insight. "The human race to which we belong, whether it is the one that is currently incarnate – or the one that is disincarnate right now, is the 'race' as the term is meant by the Guides."

"But if the races do not exist, then your Guides agree with **George Bernard Shaw** when he says – 'The American white relegates the black to the rank of shoeshine boy; and he concludes from this that the black is good for nothing but shining shoes'."

"Even though he was not evolved, Shaw realized these 'apparent' incongruities."

"Why do you question whether an intelligent man like Shaw was evolved?" Roberta asked.

"Because being very intelligent means having a 'well-organized mental body' nothing more. The evolution of which the Guides speak is the development of consciousness."

"In my opinion Shaw had the intelligence to expose all the oppressors," Roberta commented.

"Yes, but an oppressed person is not that way because others are oppressing him", Julius said, "but because he has to have the experience of being oppressed."

"Do you mean that those who oppress are doing the right thing?" Roberta said.

"Quite the contrary. The oppressor will undergo the painful experience that is his lot; nonetheless, the oppressed do not suffer in vain because they too are subject to the Law, which is perfect."

"I don't understand," Roberta gave up.

"If one does not accept the higher logic of the Guides, it is not easy to understand; in fact, it's impossible. The Guides say that if I am incarnated as part of an oppressed people and as a consequence I have the experience of being oppressed, my incarnation has not come about by chance because, for my subsequent evolution, I had to have that experience. By the same token, the one who oppresses me will, in turn, undergo a pain that 'vibrationally' will be the equivalent of the pain of the oppressed. But, listen closely – even if my oppressor chooses not to be an oppressor, I will still have the experience of being oppressed."

"So who would be your oppressor?"

"Another creature, but *in any case* I would be oppressed. This concept can be understood only if one accepts the 'mathematical structure of Reality' of which the Guides speak, a structure that, precisely because it is mathematical, does not permit someone to suffer unjustly.

"Then **Hegel**'s saying '*Fiat iustitia ne pereat mundus*' – 'Let justice be done that the world not perish' – is wrong", said Roberta, "because the world already has all the justice possible."

"Perfect. The world already has all the justice that its *average degree of evolution* allows it to have," Julius said. "I see that you are starting to use this teaching."

"Hegel's words", Roberta added, "are a paraphrase of the motto of **Holy Roman Emperor Ferdinand I** –'*Fiat iustitia et pereat mundus*' – 'Let justice be done, and the world perish.' While Ferdinand I may have been saying that the most important thing was divine justice, and that so long as this was achieved, the world could even perish, Hegel stated that only the achievement of justice would keep the world from perishing."

"You see", said Julius, "from the standpoint of the Guides' teaching, neither Hegel nor Ferdinand I is right because the world does not perish either with justice or without it, in that Reality never fails, since it is a crucible of experiences, all of which lead to evolution. In fact, whoever achieves evolution, that is to say becomes just, leaves this reality behind. Nonetheless this reality does not disappear, because it is necessary for those who still have to discover themselves to be just."

They fell silent for a few moments. Then finally they walked over to a group of colleagues to comment on the new dry-cleaning machine.

THE EARTH

More than sales representatives, Roberta and Julius seemed like two philosophers devoted to the boldest kind of speculation. Perhaps for this reason, whenever their itinerary allowed, they would stop at a place called Cimadamore, well-known because in the Middle Ages it was the refuge of some mystics. They passed through Cimadamore one year, on Columbus Day, 12th October, a national holiday for Americans. Stimulated by the place and the occasion, Roberta remembered a more or less unknown saying of **Christopher Columbus**. "The earth is not much, nor is it as big as the masses think," she quoted. "Maybe Columbus meant that man has to discover that nothing is too big for him, that nothing is beyond his measure."

"I think, instead, that Columbus intuited that the Earth, and the physical plane in general, is a minimal portion of the 'so-called worlds of perception' – which are the physical plane, the astral plane, and the mental plane. By 'masses', perhaps he meant the 'common knowledge' of those who still are in the 'middle' ranks of evolution.

Once again, Roberta noted that Julius's comments on the thought of the Greats began where her comment left off; this reflection on one hand bothered her but on the other it stimulated her to know more and more about the Guides' teaching, which revealed a reality that she had never imagined. She remembered something **Proust** had said about reality "*La réalité ne se forme que dans la mémoire.*"

Julius finally translated it himself "Reality takes shape in memory alone."

"In your opinion, what does this mean?" Roberta asked.

"If by 'memory' Proust meant the memory of the *mental body*, which is renewed at every incarnation, this is in conflict with the teaching. If, instead, by 'memory' Proust meant the degree of constitution of the consciousness, which is man's only immortal body, then he had a strong insight. In fact, our experiences are never objective, that is to say, they are not reality but only our reality, which takes shape when our inner being projects our life."

Roberta seemed to accept the answer and opened her handbag. She took out a book with a white cover entitled *The Book of Eastern Wisdom*. She read at random: "Water that is too pure has no fish."

"What do you think this means?" she said.

"It depends," Julius said. "If water represents existence, it can mean that an existence devoid of effective experiences does not produce much evolution, that is to say 'it has no fish'. It is no coincidence that Eastern spirituality is much more ancient than Western; nonetheless, both Eastern and Western spirituality are part of the General Discourse on Wisdom."

"Then your Guides make no distinction between Eastern and Western spirituality and the religions of every civilization?"

"How could they? The Guides take only evolution into consideration, not the clothing that covers it. This is why they speak of the 'General Discourse on Wisdom'."

"Listen to this **Zen koan**," said Roberta, thumbing through the book. "*Koan* is a Japanese term which literally means 'public notice'. In Zen, a koan is a formulation taken from a Sutra or an exposition of Zen experience which refers back to ultimate reality. 'Sutra' means 'guiding thread' and consists of an aphorism derived from the sacred texts, which without commentary remains more or less incomprehensible."

She read:

A mother asked her little girl:
"How much do you love me?"
The little girl replied:
"As much as the whole world
As far as the sun."

"How do you interpret this wisdom?" Julius asked.

"I don't know; maybe the koan's meaning lies in the line: 'As much as the whole world as far as the sun'?"

"That's what I think too," Julius said. "When the love that one is able to express extends for 'the whole world as far as the sun' – it means that this person has achieved a 'cosmic feeling' which is the maximum feeling attainable by an incarnate being."

Roberta watched Julius's expression as he said these words, and once again she noted his love for the Guides. She witnessed the strength her colleague drew from his faith and, at the same time, that he remained detached from it.

As though reading her mind, Julius said "You believe that I 'do not feel' what I am telling you, right?"

"I believe that you believe", Roberta answered, "and that is enough for me."

"If it is truly as you say, the Guides would say that the littleness of my faith is useful to you," said Julius.

They had stopped in the little town square of Cimadamore, crowded with people and vendors' stalls. It was a nice day and conversation was pleasant.

"Do you think Barsotti will decide in favour of the 624?" Roberta suddenly asked, referring to a model of a dry-cleaning machine that a local merchant was supposed to buy. Their conversations split between the quotidian and the transcendent, so much so that one day Roberta had said "If we go on like this, we risk going cross-eyed," – alluding to the effort they made to talk about the Guides' teaching and immediately afterwards to sell dry-cleaning machines.

They crossed the square and reached a little bridge that opened onto the valley over which Cimadamore looked. Mist was lifting under the noonday sun. Roberta paged through *The Book of Eastern Wisdom* again and stopped at a page featuring the poet **P'angyun**.

"Look how well suited these lines are to this great show on nature's part," she said:

> *What a supernatural wonder*
> *And what a miracle this is!*
> *I draw water from the well*
> *And carry firewood!*

"It's true!" Julius agreed. "They cry out that everything is a miracle."

"Miracle in what sense?" Roberta said.

"In the sense that all of life, in its most common aspects, produces evolution, that is to say, the miracle of understanding."

"Which consists in…"

"In going beyond the 'evolutive period called man' and beginning a new spiritual cycle," Julius answered.

They started down a little country lane that led out of the town and were soon immersed in deep green shade. They walked along through the scotch broom and olive trees until they reached the slopes of Mount Nanetto, where three centuries earlier an ascetic named Lallera had lived, who had been greatly loved by the local inhabitants. They entered the stone hut that the City of Cimadamore had rebuilt in the hermit's memory and read a marble plaque: "Here for seventy years lived Lallera, an ascetic of flowers and birds."

"This Lallera must have understood everything about life," Roberta commented.

"Everything or hardly anything," said Julius.

"What do you mean, hardly anything? A person so detached from material things must have understood everything about life."

"What if he was a person detached from material things but also from other people?" Julius said. "Someone can abandon society, not because he is moving on a higher plane of consciousness, which pushes us toward an exclusive contact with the Absolute, but in order to escape from other people because he feels superior or inferior to them; then his mysticism tries to demonstrate a degree of evolution that he does not possess."

"So Saint Francis, who lived a great part of his life in a hermitage, felt superior to others?" Roberta found.

"For the Guides, Saint Francis was evolved but for this reason – it is true that he lived a large part of his life as a hermit and only rarely went out into the crowds, but it is also true that, even though living in solitude, he participated in a state of consciousness of union, communion, fusion with others. In reality, he no longer needed to live with others in order to 'feel them' in every instant of his life. It is no coincidence that the individual whom we know as Saint Francis now participates in the 'cosmic state of consciousness', in other words, he has abandoned the cycle of rebirths."

"What is the cosmic state of consciousness? Roberta asked.

"It is the state of consciousness in which the individual is no longer an 'individualized' spirit but is a 'cosmic spirit' because he has transcended being human."

"I don't understand."

"Imagine an ocean and all the drops of water into which the ocean can be divided," said Julius. "Now imagine that the ocean is the state of cosmic consciousness, and we are the water drops that make up the ocean, in our current state of evolution in which we feel ourselves to be separate from each other. Well, the person whom we remember as Saint Francis *no longer feels like a drop of water in the ocean* now because he *is* the ocean; how did he reach this way of feeling? By loving Everything.

"But how?"

"Is there a person you love more than anything in your life?" Julius said.

"Yes, since I don't have children, my little niece."

"What binds you to her?"

"The love I feel for her."

"Yes, but what is this love?"

"Maybe it's the state of consciousness you were talking about?"

"Good, we agree on the fact that love is a state of consciousness. Now imagine that you want to make me feel towards your little niece the same state of consciousness that you feel towards her and that we have called 'love.' Is this possible?"

"I don't think so…"

"Why?"

"Because it is a feeling that only I have."

"And why do only you have it?"

"I don't know…"

"You are the only one who feels it because when you think about your niece, your akashic body or consciousness vibrates in a way that is exclusively your own and cannot belong to anyone else. Your rules of vibration, your 'codes' cannot be felt by anyone but you. So then, if a state of consciousness as widespread as the kind that binds you to your niece is already so incommunicable and can be believed only by the person participating in it, how can one communicate a state of consciousness in which one loves Everything? Only *the one who is it* can believe it; this is why no evolved person, no saint, no mystic could ever explain what he or she is living."

Roberta moved away a little from the stone hut that had been Lallera's home. Certainly, every time she talked with Julius she recognized many things that he said – 'recognize' was the right word because it seemed to Roberta that she had already 'heard' the concepts Julius was expressing. Or was all this an illusion? She asked herself this question while she opened *The Book of Eastern Wisdom*. She read at random a Buddhist proverb: "When the student is ready, the teacher appears."

"What do you think this means?"

Julius was one jump ahead of her,"If the student is ready to learn, he encounters the teacher."

"Yes, but what Teacher?"

"A teacher who is that for the student."

"And where does he meet him?"

"Anywhere, in a religion, in the street, in a yoga studio, anywhere."

"This is where the mistake lies," said Julius. "The true Teacher is not everywhere, but in only one place."

"Where?"

"In each person's innermost being."

In an instant, Roberta thought about all the thousands of books she had read. "Then the teacher of whom you speak is not even in culture?" she said.

"How could he be in culture? Culture is only a game played by the mind, while the 'teacher' of whom the Guides speak is a *living in consciousness* and not in the mind."

"Then what is culture good for?"

"It is good for understanding that culture is not good for anything."

"I don't understand…"

"This is not a play on words. The experience called 'culture' is useful to make the individual understand that culture is not useful for 'being,' because evolution is a state of consciousness, while culture is a *state of knowledge.*

"And what gives us this knowledge?"

"The *mind,* while the true *being* for which we all strive is 'consciousness'.

"Could you meet me halfway", Roberta gave in, "and tell me what this blessed consciousness really is?"

"The consciousness, or akashic body, is made up of the *material of the akashic plane*, just as our physical body is made up of the material of the physical plane. The difference between the two 'bodies' lies in the fact that the physical body is mortal and is made new at each incarnation – until the individual no longer needs to be reincarnated because he has achieved his evolution; consciousness is constituted, instead, through the incarnations and is immortal."

"All this is really hard to accept!" Roberta said.

"It's hard because, in the best of cases, these ideas are 'accepted', as you say, but not understood. In fact, accepting a hypothesis about reality – such as the teaching of the Guides, is a process of the mind and not of the consciousness; understanding, on the other hand, is a process of the consciousness. In short, it's a vicious circle."

"I don't understand why your Guides do not convince us of their existence with some proof," said Roberta.

"Because the 'average' evolution of mankind does not yet allow human beings to receive proof of the existence of the Beyond."

"When will we receive this proof?"

"As I said – when mankind's average evolution will let us. Then everyone will accept the medium's powers that, with numerous modifications, will become the new priestly science, which will be celebrated only in the innermost being of every person."

"I don't understand…"

"The new priestly science is what will take the place of religions. For most people now, religions are still the exclusive outposts of the afterlife, the only customs we go through on our way from and to the 'higher planes of existence'. This will no longer be the case because spiritual progress will mark the end of the function that religions have fulfilled."

They were now going back towards Cimadamore, perched on the hill, with its stone houses like a multi-coloured crowd. They were walking slowly and soundlessly.

"Who knows how much history these stones have witnessed," said Roberta, enjoying the wisdom of those impervious alleyways.

"What if that is not so?" said Julius. They had stopped in the middle of a meadow full of greenery, at the foot of a hill that held Cimadamore suspended in the sky.

"Do you mean to say that these houses and alleys have not witnessed the history we come from?" Roberta said.

"Exactly: the stones of these houses and streets are not the same ones that witnessed the events of which history speaks."

"I still don't understand," Roberta said.

"To understand it might be helpful to imagine a film that captured, let's say, the Coliseum at the moment of its greatest splendour, when thousands of individuals met their deaths, devoured by wild animals.

"Now imagine this same film running uninterruptedly to our own day, capturing the ruins of the Coliseum. Can you say that *these* stones, *this Coliseum*, are the same as those in the film made in the time of ancient Rome?"

"Of course!" Roberta said.

"Well, for the Guides this is not the case", Julius said, "because the frames of the film that contained the stones and the Coliseum are *different* frames which captured *different stones* and a *different* Coliseum, not the same as the stones and Coliseum we see now. This is why the Guides repeat that no monument, none at all that we admire today is the same as the one we consider to be the witness of memorable events. And this is true also of the monuments of our own personal life, our house or our town."

They had reached the town square of Cimadamore, where a little church invited them into its welcoming shade. They stopped talking about the Guides and approached the church, thinking about their work but always careful not to give it too much space. How much space should they give their work? Julius had asked the Guides this question, and the Guides had put before any work the only end for which man becomes an incarnate being, which is the *constitution of consciousness*. If the only purpose of human incarnations, they had said, is the constitution of consciousness and the only key to reaching it is altruistic intent, what sense does it make to give importance to work itself – and not to *how* one works, the *intent* with which one works?

"Can you give me an example of how someone should work?" asked Roberta, who had already stopped thinking about customers.

"Sure. Take a physician," Julius said. "A physician can live his profession in a 'broad' sense – that is to say, with little consciousness – seeking to further his career and become well-known, or he can live it in the right way, that is to say as an evolved person, using his work to serve others, to feel at one with others."

"I understand the physician", Roberta said, "but I do not understand how a bellboy can elevate his work."

"This is where you are wrong," Julius said. "You always have to look for the *intention*. If the bellboy does his job not just earn money, but to give satisfaction to the people who trust him with their bags; to serve a customer he doesn't even know to the best of his ability, then even a bellboy can perform his job the 'right' way."

Roberta stopped at the entrance to the church. "Then everything lies in the intention," she said.

"Intention is everything. This is why the Guides explain that man *is consciousness that reveals itself.* How? Through the quality of the intention."

Inside the church they were wrapped in a cool dampness amid the glitter of gold frames. On the first altar nearest the door, candles bathed the face of a papier-mâché Madonna in flickering light.

Roberta commented, "Here is paganism in the solid state."

"Don't worry", Julius said, "because everything is useful to the believer. If there are people who achieve a contact with God through candles and the Madonna, this too is right."

"But your Guides have said that our evolutive future does not belong to any religion and thus not to any organization," Roberta said.

"That's true, no one who has reached the evolved state of consciousness has ever done so thanks to an organization; in this case they reached it *by way of* an organization."

"What's the difference?"

"A saint, an evolved person can have reached the state of consciousness that the Guides call 'cosmic feeling' through the organization called, for example, Catholic Church – but he reached it *through it*, not *because he belonged* to that organization. It is the same for a Muslim, a Buddhist, a Hindu, an atheist, anyone who reaches the state of consciousness of the evolved."

"Because what matters is only the innermost being?" Roberta asked.

"Only the innermost being counts, the state of consciousness in which our innermost being moves. From this, for someone who has understood, they will derive the uselessness of wearing a spiritual uniform, of whatever type it may be. It is not the uniform of a spiritual organization that makes you evolved, but the state of consciousness in which you move *inside or outside* any organization. This is why the Guides reiterate, that for the Law, the only organization that matters is the one operating in our innermost being."

They sat down in a pew and remained silent in front of the altar.

After a while, Roberta opened *The Book of Eastern Wisdom* again and said "Then this is why **Fen-Yang** wrote: 'The Guides open the door but you have to enter it on your own'."

Julius met her halfway. "Do you see", he said, "how the General Discourse on Wisdom is interconnected in its essential lines? Do you see how for all the evolved of all times and religions, the essential thing is the metamorphosis that takes place inside us, the 'Great Work' of which the alchemists speak?"

"It doesn't seem to me that Fen-Yang says this," Roberta said.

"It seems to me that his maxim expresses just this – the Guide opens the door, but cannot take the place of the evolving person, who has to enter and make his way on his own."

They sat in silence.

Roberta recognized that sometimes human wisdom, which was the lodestar of her life, converged with what Julius called 'superhuman wisdom', but was this truly superhuman wisdom? She admitted that sometimes the wisdom to which Julius appealed gave answers that human wisdom did not even glimpse, and since they were in a church, she thought of prayer. She remembered what **Fedor Dostoevsky** has his character Zosima say about prayer in *The Brothers Karamazov*. She could not remember the exact words, but she did remember the essential concept. Zosima tells the youngest Karamazov brother, Alyosha that he must think of prayer as education because through communication with God, man comes to know himself.

"What do you think about this?" Roberta said.

Julius jumped. "What do I think about it?" he said absentmindedly. Then he gathered his thoughts and answered "I do not believe that prayer can ever be education but is feeling, because true prayer is the voice of the consciousness, and only when it is this does it have effect. This is why the prayer that says 'I am in Him, who is love,' is the highest there is. Every time we send a loving thought to a creature, we pray; however, this is a possibility for very few people, who are capable of not reciting devotion to the divine. This is why the Guides repeat that a person does not come to know himself through communication with God but, on the contrary, he reaches communication with God through *know thyself*. In Reality, it is the innermost being that leads the mystic to ecstasy."

They were still in the half-shadow of the church.

Slowly, the place suggested to Roberta something **Camillo Benso di Cavour** had said: "A free Church in a free State. What comment would your Guides make on this saying?" she asked.

"What comment do you think they would make?" Julius asked her back.

"Maybe they would appeal to the principle of the division of roles."

"I believe instead that they would use Cavour's words to announce the evolutive future of mankind, in which there will no longer be room for any religious organization, which will have run its course. As has already happened in the societies of our 'space brothers' who reach Earth with their vehicles that we call UFOs."

"What will replace religious organizations?"

"The marvellous product of evolution, that is to say, consciousness."

Roberta was silent and looked at the main altar.

"So religions are destined to disappear?" she said.

"Like everything that has served its purpose. Little by little, as individual and collective consciousness broadens, many received truths, such as dogmas, the virginity of Mary, papal infallibility, baptism, confirmation, the Sacra Rota, etc., will be seen for what, in effect, they are – illusions, useful for those who still need them, but these are growing fewer and fewer."

"Who are the ones who need to believe these things?"

"Those who for their evolutive needs still have to refer to an organization, a religious party, a power outside themselves, those who have not yet perceived that the religion of the future will be in each person's innermost being."

They came out of the church and headed towards the car, this time to start working. After a few miles, they reached a nearby town and entered the shop of a probable customer.

This man had been wavering for some time whether or not to buy a dry-cleaning machine made by their company or to buy from a competitor. The man was busy and had them wait, standing up, in a far corner of the shop, as often happens with sales reps.

Julius took advantage of the situation to ask Roberta something he had been wanting to ask her for some time. He said "You have committed to memory thousands of thoughts of Western thinkers, but you don't know Eastern thinkers nearly as well, to the point that, to quote one of them, you carry around with you a book of Eastern wisdom. Doesn't this seem to you like a paradox?"

"Maybe," Roberta accepted.

"Maybe the paradox is due to the fact that you have not 'felt' the General Discourse on Wisdom," Julius said. "You have never perceived that evolution knows no boundaries; it cannot be relegated to the West or the East... By the way, did you know that for the Guides, the East is more evolved than the West?"

"Because there is more hunger in the East?" Roberta asked bitterly.

"No, because in the East the *sense of the higher planes of existence* is omnipresent and thus the transcendent is omnipresent. In the end, what does our priest give you?" Julius said.

"He gives you advice, a suggestion..."

"Yes, but what evidence does he give you of the higher planes of existence? How does he speak to you of the world that comes after the physical world?"

"He usually doesn't talk about it."

"Of course, because the time of collective proof is still far away; but for those who are already able to perceive the existence of higher worlds, what does a priest of ours give you?"

"Well, how does the fakir demonstrate it?"

"By levitating, for example, or with collective hypnosis, clairvoyance… In India, you can find men who are true 'workers' for evolution. Even if consciousness and feeling united with the All is a different matter altogether.

"Many believe, for example, that the Americans are an evolved people and the Indians are an un-evolved people. For the Guides, instead, someone who is incarnated into our *space-time, called the United States of America*, is an individual who still belongs to the middle or the low-to-middle phase of evolution, to the point that he can be incarnated in a country like India only after having been through several incarnations in a country like the United States."

"It doesn't seem to me that the Americans have a middle degree of evolution," Roberta said.

"Middle and even low to middle," Julius confirmed. "By evolution, in effect, the Guides mean only the spiritual quality, and every evaluation has to be done on the basis of the average of the phenomenon being considered."

In the meantime, the shop owner was now ready to listen to them.

Julius spoke first while Roberta went through her briefcase in search of informational material. For Julius this was the hardest part of his job, because he had to present the product, but at the same time he must not betray the teaching which meant that he could not extol his product if he did not believe in what he was selling.

He thus limited himself to talking about the quality of the machine, not touching on its flaws. But this too felt unnatural to Julius, because his *feeling* considered omission to be a half-truth.

"I would have really liked to have a job with a fixed salary," he would say. "One that did not depend on the volume of sales, but this was not possible, so I accept being a sales rep until I retire because I am sure that all experiences evolve, especially the ones that are hardest for those living them."

Moreover, he would ask himself why, in the world of work and competition, he had always been only half-committed and why he had also been that way in his emotional life. Earlier married without children, which in any case he had never wanted, and then a widower: always half-way, between life on the physical plane and perception of the higher planes of existence, always midstream. What had made him so precarious in his relationships?

Julius usually answered himself by saying that his precariousness depended on an incomplete understanding of the teaching. He understood that he did not yet live in consciousness but in the mind, that is to say that he belonged to the 'broad zone of middle evolution' and that many other intellectual incarnations awaited him.

And yet, even if he did not live in the teaching, he could not do without living for the teaching and spreading it to whoever had need of it.

To the few people who asked him what 'intellectual incarnations' were, Julius would reply "Human incarnations develop according to three evolutive categories. The first is the category of *instinctive incarnations*, which the individual experiences when he begins to be incarnated as a man. In this zone, the individual lives the experiences that will enable him to overcome the *coarsest limitations*, the ones the masters call *instinctive limitations*. During these incarnations, the individual has to transcend anger, violence, carnality in its most brutal aspects, and all the limitations typical of the unevolved. To reach this stage, the individual needs strong experiences – *suited to the density of the limitations* which those experiences have to transcend; here we find the experiences of being a murderer, a rapist, and in general, the experiences of the densest I.

"Then the individual experiences the zone of *intellective incarnations*, which are necessary for him to overcome the *limitations produced by an I that is less coarse*, such as ambition, pride, haughtiness, etc. In this zone of existences, the individual will have the experiences that lead him to achieve high social rank and then to undergo economic or power reverses. This incarnational zone is experienced by individuals who still belong to the broad zone of 'medium evolution.'

"Then comes the zone of *supernormal incarnations*, in which the individual overcomes the *last limitations of the I* – for example living for one religion instead of another, and prepares to abandon the cycle of rebirths definitively."

If at this point someone asked him what type of experiences he thought he might have in his next incarnations, Julius answered sincerely "I am sure I will have to have experiences of Love, which will lead me to feel others are One with me and not just to *think* they are, as is the case with me now."

RULES OF EXISTENCE

In the following months, Roberta became keenly interested in Eastern wisdom, to the point that she memorized many Eastern maxims with the same zeal with which she remembered Western ones. She was especially intrigued by a concept expressed by the **Buddha**; she did not know why, but she intuited that this maxim was a compendium of Eastern wisdom.

She asked Julius "What would the Guides say about this saying by the Buddha? 'With faith, honesty, energy, with meditation and study of the law, always exercising knowledge and recollecting memory, you will overcome even the greatest pain'."

"Perhaps they would say that this saying, like many by great men, is rather vague," Julius replied. "The fame of certain sayings is often due to the fame of the person who said it, more than to the value of the saying itself."

"It seems to me to be full of meaning," Roberta said.

"The best meaning I know how to give this saying is connected with evolution in general because faith, honesty.."

"…energy, meditation, study of the law…," Roberta continued.

"…are nothing other than the rules of existence which we attain through evolution," Julius said. "Rules that in turn lead to a subsequent degree of evolution; meditation, for example, is reached because one begins to feel thought to be a dimension of existence in and of itself. It is through meditation that *one begins to live in an aware way on the astral and mental plane,* even while remaining incarnate."

"Why does the Buddha say that by following these rules one overcomes pain?" Roberta asked.

"Because evolution erases pain. In fact, pain serves to give a person understanding, to make him evolve, but when the individual has understood, he no longer needs pain."

"What do you think of this poem by **Kalidasa**, an Indian poet and playwright who lived between 350 and 420?" Roberta said, reading out this:

> *Yesterday is only a dream.*
> *Tomorrow is but a vision.*
> *But today well lived*
> *makes every yesterday a dream of happiness,*
> *and every tomorrow a vision of hope.*

"What do you think of it?" asked Julius.

"I think that every day should be faced with courage and joy."

"I'm sorry, but this is a useless explanation," said Julius. "It could be offered by any country priest or many so-called 'sages', who have gone down in history for sayings that are so totally obvious."

"So what would your Guides say about it, then?"

"They would say first and foremost that neither yesterday nor tomorrow exist, but only the *eternal present,* that is, today. Thus not only is yesterday a dream but life itself is a dream, if we consider the *limited degree of evolution* of those who still have need of life on the physical plane, to broaden their consciousness."

"Well, what about today well lived – what would they say about that?"

"That a today lived *objectively* well does not exist, because everyone lives his today as his evolution allows him to live it, therefore *well* is subjective for each person."

"What do you mean?"

"That everyone *lives his life in the best way for him*, the way permitted to him by the degree of evolution he has achieved."

"Can you give an example?"

"Take your life, for example. You were married, then separated and divorced..."

"My marriage had failed before my husband and I separated," Roberta said.

"Of course, but you are the one who let your marriage fail."

"Certainly not! My husband always betrayed me."

"Of course, but you are the one who married a man capable of betraying you."

"How did I know he would betray me? When we met, I was eighteen years old!"

"But you are the one who fell in love with the personality of your future husband, the personality that would lead him to betray you."

"But who is so wise at that age?"

"This wisdom was not yet within the reach of your *awareness on the physical plane* because *it was not yet within the reach of your consciousness.* If you, even at the age of eighteen, had had *enough consciousness,* you would not have fallen in love with your future husband. The proof is that now you would no longer fall in love with a personality like your husband's."

"That's for sure!" Roberta confirmed.

"So you see", Julius said, "you too, in the experiences called 'falling in love and marriage', behaved in the best way 'permitted' to you by the degree of evolution where you were at age nineteen. This is the way it is for everybody."

"Then it's this way for everything," Roberta replied.

"It is this way for everything," Julius repeated. "This is the *mathematical structure of reality* of which the Guides speak."

"I am truly your friend. What about you?" Roberta suddenly asked.

"I am not only your friend, *I feel you are a part of me,*" said Julius.

"Then what do you say about this way of conceiving of friendship? It is a thought by the famous Arab poet and algebraist **Omar Khayyam**. In his pronouncements in the form of tercets he denied God, evolution and in essence everything your Guides say. It follows naturally that he does not even believe in friendship." From *The Book of Eastern Wisdom,* Roberta read:

> *Look: a friendly hand reaches out to you*
> *Grasp it, then: and meanwhile ask yourself*
> *If one day it will strike you in enmity.*

"Well", said Julius, "this creature, even though he is a poet, is a spiritual illiterate, because giving friendship does not mean expecting friendship, but giving without expecting anything in return, because *for those who love, the reward is love itself.*"

"It seems to me, too, that Khayyam is a poet without hope," Roberta admitted.

"In fact, someone who does not know how to hope shows that his feeling is still insufficient," Julius said. "The Guides repeat that when we have no reason to hope, we have to hope, in order to create hope."

"What does it mean 'to create hope'?"

"To believe in a better future, *to the point of creating it.*

How can we improve our future, which is *the projection of what we are now*, if not by being better now? If the vibrations of our codes do not increase in frequency now, how can they create in the future, experiences that will demand *codes with a higher number of vibrations?*"

Roberta was quiet and very sceptical.

Julius continued "I understand that it is hard for you to accept these concepts, because you are new to the Guides' logic, but if you begin loving this teaching, over time you will learn to apply it to your life and also to that of others..."

"I try", Roberta said, "but for now I can't do it. The teaching is too far away from my nature."

"Because your nature is still too mental: it is no coincidence that for many years you had an ideology as your faith. The teaching has to be felt, not thought."

"No, I can't do it," Roberta repeated.

"Then don't force yourself. The time has not yet come for you for dropping the veil of illusion."

"The veil of illusion?..."

"Yes, the *veil of illusion and the veil of the I,* because the I is illusion. It is the illusion necessary to the evolutive period called man, but in a Reality, in which all is One, it is an illusion."

Roberta remained silent.

Then, to escape the severity of that concept, she read another maxim from *The Book of Eastern Wisdom:* **You-men.**

Every day
Is a good day.

"What do you think this maxim means?" she said.

"That every day is a better day", Julius said, "because evolution is celebrated every day. Indeed, our evolution does not depend on the intensity of the experiences that we create-perceive every day, but *how* we live these experiences."

"You mean, on the state of mind in which we live them?"

"On the *intention* with which we live them; only the intention with which we live our experiences uses their *evolutive proportion*."

"Evolutive proportion?" Roberta said.

"Yes, the *evolutive proportion* of an experience is the *evolutive message* which that experience wants to bring us," Julius explained. "For example,when you, had the motor-scooter accident that forced you to stay in bed for a month, the evolutive proportion of that experience consisted in the *expansion of feeling* that you could draw from your forced immobility and thus from the reflection and the resulting *understanding* that you could achieve, thanks to the *vibratory event* called an 'auto accident'."

"What should I have understood?"

"Only your consciousness, which *promoted* that accident, knows this. For the Guides, accidents happen in order to move the individual out of the *crystallization* into which he has fallen—to make *his astral body vibrate*—to shake his inner being with the aggression of fear, physical pain, and temporary disability."

"Do all accidents happen for this reason?" Roberta asked.

"Nothing happens by chance. Let's take a simple muscle strain. The individual who suffers one will be limited in his movements. He will feel a sharp pain every time he moves the strained muscle; reminded by the sensation of pain, he will be forced to think about the movement that caused the strain, and this will lead him to evaluate the causes. All this work can make the individual's *astral body* vibrate; it can change his *astral codes* and thus *break up some crystallizations*: move him out of a stagnant state – in a word, cause him to evolve."

"I didn't know that even the slightest incidents of our life had a higher cause," Roberta said.

"But it's true, because All is One," Julius said. "If in a container of water something moves, the entire volume of water in the container will be influenced by it. Thus we have the omnipresent law of cause and effect."

"What represents the All is One?" Roberta asked.

"The volume of water, where *both the spiritual causes that produce the accident on the physical plane and the physical plane itself coexist.*"

Roberta thought that Julius loved the Guides so much that he did not realize that, for most people's level of understanding, their teaching was an insurmountable obstacle. And yet she was sure that if one does not believe in something with all one's heart, then one cannot even think of transmitting it to others. For this reason, even if she did not understand many of the concepts that Julius was passing on to her, she was influenced by his words, as though they were not passing through her mind but by a higher path. Satisfied with this reflection, she read some lines by a Japanese poet. The commentary said that the poet was a woman renowned for her beauty.

Weeping destroys
The one who, disdainful, did not nurture
Love, which now runs from her.

"These lines seem autobiographical to me," Roberta commented.

"Maybe she speaks of love as a product of beauty, which earlier was there and then is gone," Julius said.

"For your Guides, what is beauty?" Roberta asked.

"It is the attraction exerted on others through one's *physical body*," Julius said. "Beauty, too, is a vibratory event. Someone who is born ugly very often had an attractive body in an earlier life, because each person has an experience that he had not had earlier or repeats an experience that he did not understand."

"I agree that beauty, like an actress's, can change the course of a life", Roberta said, "but I do not believe that an ordinary kind of beauty, like that of a girl you might see on the street, is important."

"Instead, the physical body's ability to attract is always very important, even if we are not aware of it, because it varies the *codes* of the people with whom we come into contact and varies our *codes* when we undergo the *effects* of the variations of *others' codes.*"

They had reached the yard of Julius's little house, which he used also to park his car. They were there to consult their list of old customers, whom they intended to call on in the absence of new ones. They climbed the stairs that led to the house and came out on a tiny porch overlooking the little yard.

"Here everything is small", Roberta thought, "except Julius's love for his Guides."

They looked out over the porch and stood for a while without speaking. Beyond the yard stretched an untilled field that, with its tangled vegetation, threatened the tidiness of Julius's little house. It looked like this raw nature was about to jump over and swallow up the house, so much so that Roberta commented on it with a saying attributed to the famous Swedish naturalist **Carl Linnaeus**: *"Natura non facit saltus."*

"That is a saying that has been used both by the materialists and the Guides," Julius said.

"Nature does not move by leaps," Roberta translated.

"In fact, the materialists use this saying to deny the passage from the ultra-physical world to the physical world", Julius said, "while the Guides use it to confirm that an individual's evolution advances spiritually, *without taking leaps*, through the mineral, vegetable, and animal realms, up to man and beyond."

"But in the end, this evolution, where does it move forward from?" Roberta asked.

"From the degree of consciousness of the individual which is expanding, from his ability to understand that he is *self-aware*."

"I do not believe that a mouse can have a degree of consciousness," Roberta said.

"Indeed, a mouse does not yet possess *his own* consciousness, but is the *sensor of a group soul* to which a great many other mice belong," Julius explained. "The group soul is *incarnate* in its sensors, which we call 'mice', in order to complete the *first sublevels of its own astral body* and establish its own *mental body*. Therefore consciousness already exists, even if an embryonic state, not in the individual mouse but in the *soul group* to which the mouse belongs, and not only that: the earliest beginning of what will be the *consciousness of a saint* is already present in the *mouse's soul group*.

"It is no coincidence that the Guides explain that the entire evolution of the individual goes *from the stone to the saint*."

"Your Guides speak often of sainthood..." Roberta said, her mind struggling.

"*Sainthood* understood as a state of consciousness of the evolved being, not as a religious label," Julius specified.

'Yes, I meant that secular minds, too, have perceived the greatness of sainthood," Roberta said. "**Oscar Wilde**, for example, said that the only difference between a saint and a sinner is that *every saint has a past and every sinner has a future*."

"In fact, for the Guides every saint's past is sin, and every sinner's future is sainthood," Julius agreed.

"Sainthood understood as evolution?" Roberta asked.

"Understood as evolution that each one reaches by travelling *his path*."

"Then why did you say that every saint's past is sin?"

"Because every individual who will later find himself to be a saint, evolved – Guide, leader, superman, etc., obeying the Law that compels everyone to evolve. Before becoming a saint he has moved through all the sins, all the lower grades that led him to be a saint: he has killed, betrayed, raped, tried every excess, in short, he has *built up* his sainthood brick by brick."

"When a being is no longer reincarnated, how does he live?" Roberta asked.

"He does not live in a way that we can understand. Someone who has moved beyond the evolutive period called man 'does not go to..,' 'does not come from..,' 'does not behave..,' no longer acts like a man but *feels more and more.*"

"I don't understand," Roberta said.

"Someone who is no longer a man lives by *successions of feeling*, Julius explained. "That is to say, he truly lives. On the plane of consciousness, the illusion of movement which is in force on the physical plane is replaced by the individual's gradual development *from a more restricted feeling to an increasingly amplified feeling*. This is the 'life of consciousness' of which the Guides speak."

"I still don't understand," Roberta said. "What is this 'increasingly amplified feeling' – how does it work?"

"It means participating in an ever wider part of Reality, 'being' an ever increasing number of individuals. An 'increasingly amplified feeling' means 'feeling oneself to be also the other', as happens to the evolved being on the physical plane, but more, much, much more."

"But, in the end, who regulates all this perfection?" Roberta asked. "Who makes everything go the way it should go and keeps reality from falling apart?"

"The *archetypes*...," Julius replied.

They were sitting on the porch of Julius's little house, where everything reflected the moderation in which he lived; there only their thoughts were grand.

Getting up from his lounge chair, Julius said softly "The *individual archetype* is the state of consciousness which sets the boundaries within which an individual's set of codes can vary." Then, trusting too much to Roberta's powers of understanding, he continued "An *individual code* differs from another, but it never goes beyond the existing content of the *cosmic archetype* that, in the form of a *mathematical model*, takes *numeric codes*, that is to say takes its own specific *archetypal code* from the *general archetype,* which is the direct emanation of the Principle."

"I did not understand a thing," Roberta said, disappointing him.

"Are you familiar with the instrument that in electrical terms is called the rectifier?" Julius went on. "The rectifier is an electrical device that keeps the quantity of electrical current constant, without being too weak or too strong, but works so that there may be constancy, *a constant*. Well, the *general archetype* keeps the density of *what is emanated* constant, but this does not mean unchanging. The *general archetype* establishes the various bands: it establishes the band of the various *cosmic archetypes*, the bands of the various *individual archetypes*. The *general archetype* is what gives a sense of *vibratory distance* to the All."

"Can you give me an example?" Roberta surrendered.

"I'll take the example of a tree, which is the same example the Guides give. One could say about a tree that the branches are the various *personalities* located on the countless levels of the archetype. The trunk is the *individual consciousness and sensations and thoughts*, thus the *astral and mental body.* The tree's root is the spirit, w*hile the ground where the root is sunk is the 'Tau plane'.* But the water, which keeps the soil fixed in this density in which the tree grows, develops and dies – assuming that this can be true for an individual – is the Absolute, is God, is the *Principle*, or to put it better, the *Principle through the general archetype.*"

"Wait a second," Roberta gasped. "What do your Guides mean by personality?"

"You are a personality, I am one, every individual 'puts on' a personality that varies with each incarnation."

"Then **Max Jacob** is wrong", Roberta sighed, "when in *Art Poetique* he states that a personality is nothing other than an error that endures."

"In fact, personality could be an error that endures if consciousness did not change personality with each incarnation. Instead, we have seen that consciousness is the trunk of a tree and the branches are the various personalities, therefore a personality is never an error, but is an individual's way of being; it is a state of consciousness that, as such, must be lived. The Guides explain that the personality never remains the same, because at every incarnation the individual lives *the worlds of perception, that is to say the physical, astral, and mental planes*, with different *codes*. In other words with a different personality, suited to making him achieve a broader evolution compared to the previous incarnation."

"Can you give me an example?"

"Let's take the case of extreme personalities, those in which the individual has the experience, let's say, of a religious and in the next life, of a playboy. These personalities are characteristic of *medium evolution,* in which the individual does not yet have a sufficiently established consciousness and so he 'fibrillates' from one experience to another which is its opposite, because he lacks the inner balance given by a more advanced evolution."

"You always talk about evolution, the law of cause and effect and the mathematical structure of reality", Roberta said, "however, **Jacques Monod** says in *Chance and Necessity,* 'Pure chance, chance alone, free but blind freedom, at the very root of the prodigious edifice of evolution – today this central notion of biology is no longer an hypothesis among the many possible or at leave conceivable, but is the only one conceivable in that it is the only one compatible with reality as revealed to us by observation and experience.' What would your Guides say about this idea?"

"They would say this: what Monod calls 'chance', for the Guides is instead *nature proceeding by attempts,* which should not be interpreted as an *unconscious automatism* but as a *process continuously controlled by the law of evolution.*"

"Can you give me an example?"

The example the Guides give: if a blind man has to reach a certain place without someone to lead him, he will proceed by attempts. This means that first he will make a mistake, then another mistake, then he'll go back, then he'll go forward, he'll change direction, but in the end he will arrive at the place where he has to go. The Law proceeds in the same way: by attempts. This does not mean that, as Monod says, chance exists, but that, on the contrary, everything is regulated by a *perfect finalism.*"

Julius sat back down on the lounge chair and added, "In true reality, chance does not exist."

"Because everything is foreseen?" Roberta said.

"Yes, but everything is foreseen because it already exists!"

With two strides Roberta crossed Julius's little porch and took from her jacket her notebook filled with jottings. She leafed through it intently. Julius did not understand why a woman still young and attractive like Roberta spent a large part of her life selecting, studying, and filing away the thoughts of the Greats. And yet he too, and much earlier than Roberta, had collected and studied the teachings of the Guides.

"**Frederick the Great** also talks about chance in the *Letter to Voltaire*," said Roberta, reading from her notebook. "Listen to what he says 'The older one gets the more one is convinced that His Sacred Majesty Chance does three-quarters of the work in this miserable universe'."

"The Guides would not agree with Frederick the Great either," Julius immediately said. "They would not for two reasons: first, because this universe is not miserable, but is the best creation-perception that our *collective individuality* can live in relative to its level of evolution. Second, because chance does not do three-quarters of the work in this universe: chance does not even do any work, because it does not exist. In Reality, what is commonly called chance are the *steps in the individual and collective evolutive equation*."

"Are you referring to the blind man's attempts you were talking about earlier?" Roberta said.

"Exactly! I see that you are beginning to get into the teaching."

"Certainly, you have no doubts!" Roberta said. "You really could teach."

"In what sense?" Julius asked.

"In the sense **Goethe** talks about in *Faust*, when he states that only someone who has no doubts can teach. Goethe says:

Heed not the one who expresses doubt to you;
Teaching is forbidden him, since he doubts.
One who presumes to teach must give something."

"I have to disappoint you, because I have many doubts, which I always check against the grid of the teaching. Then, it's true, I also have faith, because the answers that the teaching gives me nourish my faith, but that's something different."

"Yes, but what would you say about Goethe's lines?" Roberta asked.

"The spiritual seeker must have doubts, because he has to be open to all the possible truths; this is the honest way of acting. The Guides urge anyone who is witness to their teaching to express their doubts openly, and they will resolve them if they are doubts and not prejudices. Therefore it is not true that, if one has doubts and teaches, one gives nothing to those who are learning. Quite the reverse is true: doubts are useful to both those who teach and those who are learning, to delve more deeply into the question."

"You always talk about teaching", Roberta said, "but have you ever thought that you might seem like a slave to the teaching? Listen to what **Montesquieu** says in his *Essay on the Causes that can Influence the Spirit and the Character*: 'A man who teaches can easily become stubborn, because he practices the profession of someone who is never wrong.' Would you be capable of some self-criticism?"

"You see", Julius said, "I do not do anything other than report my interpretation of the teaching dispensed by the Guides, in a manner that is organized over the years, that's all."

"So you do not commit the sin of fanaticism?"

"Maybe I do, but that is not my intention, perhaps my love.

for the Guides can seem fanatical, and I apologize for that, but I do not do anything other than pass along a teaching that is not mine."

"So then you do not believe **Keats**'s lines from *The Fall of Hyperion* pertain to you?

> *Fanatics have their dreams, wherewith they weave*
> *A paradise for a sect.*"

"No, I don't think they do, because I can admit that mediumship does not exist and that the Guides do not exist. But my love would remain for what I believe is the quality of the teaching, whatever its origin; nonetheless it is true that in mediumship there is the constant danger that sects may form."

"How?"

"Someone who participates seriously in a phenomenon with a medium often becomes convinced that only that phenomenon is genuine and that only through that instrument are important teachings dispensed. Afterwards, it could happen that the participants become followers of the medium, and later still, that the medium acts like a Guide. In that case it is the ego of the instrument that triumphs."

"What should happen instead?"

"That the instrument feels itself to be what it is in Reality, that is to say a mere *tessera* in an overall *evolutive mosaic*."

"Why do you call it an 'evolutive mosaic'?"

"Because the development of mediumship obeys an overall evolutive design; by *evolutive mosaic* the Guides mean the phenomenon by which mediumship progressively spreads. The phenomenon is allowed naturally by the evolution achieved by mankind itself and happens in order to promote a new evolution."

"Why is it a *mosaic*?"

"Because mediumship is made up of as many *tesserae* as there are mediums operating in the world, both in the West and in the East – note this! – *where meditation is the equivalent of a trance.*"

SICKNESS

They looked over the list of Julius's old customers and decided to phone a man of the church who years before had bought an industrial washing machine. He ran a home where many disabled people lived and perhaps he might need a new machine.

The home was called 'Guance Rosse', which was the name of the place where the home was located.

Roberta and Julius waited in the entrance hall until the director could receive them. While they waited, they watched the passing to and fro of the home's disabled guests, a traffic of suffering which they would never have imagined could be so ordinary and usual.

After a while Roberta said "I don't understand how **Epicurus** could say in his *Sovereign Maxims* that prolonged illnesses give the flesh more pleasure than pain."

"It depends on how one looks at life," Julius observed. "Epicurus looked at life solely from the standpoint of pleasure. For the Guides, instead, prolonged illnesses are the instruments of the Law which produce pain and thus evolution, in a specialized way."

"So Epicurus was wrong?"

"No one is wrong. Epicurus simply lived his evolution, which enabled him to have that view of life and not another one. You see", Julius added, "what man calls *happiness*, for the Guides is only satisfaction because according to their teaching, happiness cannot be achieved in the human *evolutive period. Human feeling* is still far away from fusion with other beings, which is the only state of consciousness that enables access to happiness."

"I don't understand how satisfaction can take the place of happiness," Roberta said.

"It is possible if one temporarily satisfies one's I, which thus has the *impression of happiness*, but not happiness. The I, in fact, being *separateness*, is illusion."

"Can you explain that better?" Roberta said.

"Let's take success, for example, which is a great object of worship for the I. Someone who achieves success is not happy, but fills a dissatisfaction with a *temporary satisfaction* which will last until his I digs other craters of dissatisfaction. This is why the Guides repeat that the I cannot bring happiness, because it always wants something *for itself,* while the evolved being, which has consumed its I, wants something for others."

"Then your Guides would agree with the elder **Alexandre Dumas** when he said in *Le Corricolo* 'I do not believe there is anything better than success to heal one of pride'."

"Indeed, the Guides would agree with Dumas because they repeat that it is necessary *to experience in order to become saturated.*"

"I don't understand," Roberta said.

"The phrase *to experience in order to become saturated* means that, in order to overcome a limitation that imposes certain experiences, it is necessary to repeat those experiences until one is fed up with them, and no longer needs them because the *limitation* that made us create-perceive those experiences has been transcended."

"Then would Dumas's words mean that if success is sought after by one's pride, there is nothing more effective than experiencing success for transcending pride?"

"That's exactly right," Julius said.

They were interrupted by the director of Guance Rosse, who came towards them, smiling. He was a man about fifty years old, wearing a clerical collar. He led them into his office, a modest room but with an air of great efficiency. The director spoke briefly and effectively. He specified the characteristics of the washer he intended to buy and then invited the two sales representatives to take a tour of the Guance Rosse facilities.

They walked through a building with numerous rooms, in each of which lived a disabled person. Some of these looked out the door and greeted them as they walked past. Roberta was disturbed by the suffering of these people and took advantage of a moment when the director had walked away to whisper to Julius "What would your Guides say about the way **Rex Stout**, the creator of Nero Wolfe, viewed guests, who were certainly very different from these? Stout has Wolfe say: 'A guest is a jewel resting on the cushion of hospitality'."

"Perhaps they would say that for the evolved being, there are no guests, therefore no cushions to rest them on", said Julius, "because for the evolved, *others are the constant guests of his life*. Besides, let's not forget that the evolved being is such, precisely because he moves on this plane of consciousness."

The director returned and they crossed some more rooms until they came to the entrance to the home's chapel. Here the director knelt and remained for a few minutes in prayer.

Roberta whispered into Julius's ear "According to **Pascoli**, this director would be the height of evolution…"

"Why?" Julius asked.

"Because in the *Nuovi Poemetti* Pascoli says 'Someone who prays is a saint, but one who acts is more of a saint.' It seems to me that this priest does both."

"Maybe so," said Julius. "But before giving someone the title of evolved being, we would have to know his intention in performing that action, which to us seems altruistic. If the director is acting like this in order to further his career in heaven, then his act is not that of an evolved being. The value of the act is given only by the *intention with which that act is performed.* Therefore what Pascoli says, 'One who acts is more of a saint,' is right in proportion to the *quality of the intention* with which one acts.

"Then one who prays is more of a saint", Roberta said, "because he appeals only to the intention."

"Here too we have to look at the intention with which he prays. Many have abandoned the world and taken refuge in prayer in order to appear great in the eyes of men, to stand out in their spiritual career, for who is greater than a saint?"

They fell silent as the director stood up from his prayer bench.

"Forgive me", he said, "but I needed a moment of recollection. At Guance Rosse every day, we are on the front line."

They continued their tour of the home, and Roberta said, "Excuse me, Father, may I ask you a personal question?"

"Certainly," he replied.

"You who are so deeply involved in life, do you still believe in the virginity of Our Lady?"

The man hesitated a moment. Perhaps that question recalled to him ancient torments.

"I will answer you immediately", he said, "just as soon as I ask Marietta if she has done her blood work." He walked over to a young girl who was playing ping-pong from her wheelchair.

Roberta and Julius saw how the director talked to Marietta lovingly and how the girl caressed him with her eyes. Then he came back over to them and started talking about other things.

But Roberta was insistent "Pardon me, Father, do you believe in Mary's virginity?" Then she added, "Surely you do not share **Voltaire**'s opinion, when in *Le Sottisier* he wrote: 'It is one of the superstitions of the human mind to have imagined that virginity could be a virtue'."

In the end the director gave in "You see when you work in places like this, you don't ask yourself these questions. Look at Marietta, for example, such a beautiful soul and such an immobile body…"

"I took the liberty of asking this question", Roberta explained, "because I do not understand how you, who are so useful to others, still need to believe in Mary's virginity to feel you are useful."

The director still evaded the question. "Well", he said, "in a certain sense I do believe." It was evident that the director, without any feeling, was defending a dogma of his organization.

Afterwards, they visited with many other people like Marietta, and their tour of Guance Rosse came to an end. The two sales representatives came out into the open air.

"Who knows what your Guides would say about a person like the director," Roberta commented.

"I believe that they would approve, even if the intention with which he carries out his function is not completely altruistic," Julius said.

"How can the intention with which he does this job not be altruistic?"

"It depends on the individual. We have already talked about this. One can act altruistically in order to be considered spiritually great, without having an altruistic intent. In this case, the individual is living still sunken in *becoming,* that is to say in illusion, and not yet living in *being.*"

"Then why did you say that the Guides would approve of him?" Roberta asked.

"Because an individual who carries out a function like the director's, even if he does not do it with an altruistic intent, nonetheless does good to other people. He does not live a sterile life like those who withdraw into a hermitage and are not useful to anyone."

"Then to do good the director did not need to wear a clerical collar, that is to say, a uniform," Roberta said.

"Exactly, he could have done without it. We have also talked about this. When an individual has an already established consciousness, he no longer needs uniforms in order to love. He no longer needs to belong to an organization. Nonetheless, if the individual put on a uniform in order to love, it is a sign that he still has to have the experience of the uniform."

They got into the car and slowly drove away from Guance Rosse.

SWALLOWING UP FILM FRAMES

Their work was done by appointment, which hardly ever resulted in a solid contract after the first meeting and relied on repeated actions, which required planning. This made Roberta think of something **Suetonius** had said.

"In *Divus Augustus*, Suetonius has Augustus say, '*Festina lente.*' Make haste slowly. Doesn't it seem to you that this saying is a good commentary on our work?"

"Everything is a commentary on everything, because All is One," Julius admitted. "Suetonius was probably referring to an inner balance which Augustus possessed. For the Guides, too, anxiousness and hurry are never a sign of evolution, because they steal time away from reflection, which is the true driving force of consciousness."

Roberta nodded and took her notebook out of her pocket. She read out something **Hemingway** had said:

Rush, that most exciting perversion of life,
the necessity of accomplishing something in less time
than should be truly allowed for its doing.

"It seems that Hemingway liked haste", she said, "that line is from *The Green Hills of Africa*."

"In any case Hemingway admits that haste is a perversion of life," Julius said, putting both hands on the steering wheel. And for the Guides, haste often means 'swallowing up the film frames', without finding out what lies hidden behind each frame…"

"In this case, what do you mean by the film frames?" Roberta asked.

"The experiences of daily life."

"And what lies hidden behind every frame?"

"The possibility of broadening one's consciousness."

"In what way?"

"By discovering the *evolutive proportion* which every experience, even what seems the most insignificant to us, wants to teach us. We already said that the *evolutive proportion* of an experience is the evolutive message which that experience wants to give us. The rush to live, existential anxiety, causes suffering, and perhaps it is no coincidence that Hemingway experienced this perversion of life, as he called it, to the point of suicide."

They were travelling along the provincial road that leads from Alto Pascio to Riccadonna. Here they had to call on a restaurant entrepreneur who was very well-known in the area. They reached Riccadonna and drove down the town's main street, crowded with elegant shops. Among this, a little store stood out for its modesty, without a showy window, marked by the sign 'Veterinarian'.

Roberta pointed the shop out to Julius and promptly said, "Maybe it would have pleased **Gramsci** to see the humility of that shop in the midst of this exultant luxury."

"What does Gramsci have to do with it?" Julius asked.

"Gramsci loved animals, and consequently those who take care of them. In *Letters from Prison*, he wrote to Tatiana Schucht 'I have always respected physicians and medicine, although I respect veterinarians even more because they heal animals who cannot speak and describe the symptoms of their illness'. "

"It is not the case with Gramsci, but placing particular importance on *lives inferior to human life* can be a sign of a lack of understanding of the Law," Julius said. "Those who feel this way often attribute to animals a sensibility that the animals do not have. Many, in front of images documenting life in the animal kingdom, tremble with horror at the cruelty imposed by the food chain. But they do not know that the sensibility with which an animal lives the event in which it is killed is not the sensibility man attributes to it. The experience felt, for example, by a gazelle when it is torn apart by a lion is much less traumatizing than the experience we have of watching it be torn apart."

"Then why is the animal world so full of experiences that seem so cruel to us?" Roberta asked.

"Because what seems like cruelty to us humans is only the *vibratory nature* of those experiences, which have to be strong because individuals who draw evolution from them, that is the animals, are still 'individuals with a low evolution'. The lower the evolution, the greater the need for *strongly vibratory experiences so as to transcend oneself,* for events capable of *shaking up* the individual animal."

"What then would your Guides have to say about this thought from **Hippocrates** on human experience? – '*Vita brevis, ars longa, tempus praeceps, experimentum pericolosum, iudicium difficile.*' This means more or less: Life is short, art is long, the occasion fleeting, the experiment dangerous, and judgment difficult."

"Certainly they would say that Hippocrates had understood life, because life is *evolutive toil*, without which no one can evolve. Only the incarnations that the Guides call 'pauses' are effortless and are the ones in which, from the evolutive point of view, one is just marking time. But the roads not traversed have in any case to be traversed…"

"When?" Roberta asked.

"In a later life, when the individual is capable of understanding."

In the meantime they had entered a restaurant, where they were greeted by an expert bustle mixed with the faint smell of cooked food. On the walls, in place of photos of famous customers, were lined up hundreds of books of all sizes, some of them rare, according to Roberta's judgment as they sat down at a table away from the crowd. She ordered a dish that did not contain meat, and then said "How can a book that is not even able to take us beyond all books be important?"

Julius was surprised by this statement, because he knew his fellow worker to be a devoted student of the mind and thus of books, and so he asked "What brought about this mystical surrender?"

"It is not something I said," Roberta replied. "**Nietzsche** said it; it seems very profound to me."

"Without question," Julius admitted. "It is what the Guides say about culture."

"They say we can do without culture?"

"Yes, because culture means intelligence, it means the mind, while evolution has nothing to do with the mind, since it is consciousness. This is why great unschooled persons, such as Saint Joseph of Cupertino, famous for his levitations, could be great evolved beings."

Roberta was silent; her attention waned whenever they talked about a religion. Julius repeated in vain that the Guides do not favour any religion but rather proclaim the religion of the inner being. As a good student of the mind, Roberta viewed religions only as a power structure.

They started eating. Roberta chewed her pasta, thinking about something **Napoleon** had said which fitted very well their routine as travelling sales representatives: always on the road, always the same pasta.

"Do you know what Napoleon said about routine? –'It is 'fortunate that mediocrity can act only according to routine'," she said.

Julius lifted his eyes from his plate, "I didn't know that", he said, "but I do know what the Guides said about Napoleon."

"What?"

"That he had an *overdeveloped ego*, because his conquests were the brutal product of the *expansion of his ego*. He was certainly an individual with a *very well-organized mental body*, a genius in the art of war, but true evolution does not come from being a genius. Paradoxically, Napoleon belonged to that mediocrity which he detested so much."

"It seems to me that by 'mediocrity' Napoleon meant all those people who are capable of damaging others and are kept from doing so by the mediocrity of their lives," Roberta objected.

"Precisely, and didn't Napoleon act like a mediocre person would have acted? Did he not cause great grief and millions of deaths?"

They continued eating. After a while, Roberta said "Then, according to your Guides, only those who think like **Leonardo da Vinci** are right, when he said in his *Fragments* 'I never tire of helping, I never tire of serving'."

"Certainly," Julius approved. "Leonardo understood that man's evolutive future consisted in giving oneself to others, without expecting anything in return."

Like an automaton, a vagrant entered the restaurant, which was teeming with customers and waiters, and headed for the kitchen. He seemed sure of where he was going, and in fact no waiter stopped him. Roberta thought the vagrant was known in the restaurant, and immediately she associated that situation with a saying by **Victor Hugo**: "Whoever gives to the poor lends to God."

"What would your Guides say about this thought?" she said. "That it is necessary to give to the poor?"

"This is a topic about which I asked a lot of questions at a large gathering," Julius said. "How do you think the Guides answered this question?"

"I believe that charitable giving has become a compassion business," Roberta said.

"That's where you are wrong," said Julius. "As always, the solution to every doubt about a choice of behaviour lies in the intention. If I have an altruistic intention, I cannot avoid giving charity, even to someone that I know to be a parasite on society and will go spend my offering on drugs or alcohol. This means that I can decide to give because of the simple fact that this person has held out his hand to me, rightly or wrongly; but if I do not have this purity of intention, it is better for me not to give anything. In essence the Guides say – 'give to everyone, but only if you can handle it!'"

Roberta looked around her, as though to break free of this logic that intimidated her, but at the same time intrigued her. She thought that the philosophy which Julius attributed to his Guides, even if it was the fruit of the unconscious of the persons called mediums and did not come from Guides who were outside the medium, was as worthy of attention as that merited by many other philosophies which had later failed miserably.

She thought of a maxim of **Hobbes**: "In this '*Primum vivere, deinde philosophari.*' – First live, then philosophize. What would your Guides say about this criticism of philosophy made by a great philosopher?" Roberta asked.

"They would say that Hobbes had understood that philosophy is *only a path* to reach consciousness, demonstrating in this that he possessed a significant degree of evolution. In fact, recognizing that first one has to live and then to philosophize means having intuited that the goal of every life is to *live intensely* the experiences on the physical plane."

"Then philosophy is not enough?" Roberta said.

"It can't be enough, because philosophy is mind, it is the 'mental body', while the object of evolution is consciousness. It is no coincidence that many famous men, who lived in the triumph of the mind, possessed a very limited degree of evolution; in the use of the *mental body*, even as a genius, there is no evolution, which exists only in consciousness."

A beautiful woman walked into the restaurant. Roberta was distracted from Julius's final words and fixed her attention on that lithe body, which moved almost ceremoniously, as though immersed in a dense, fragrant oil. The woman sat down with some other people a short distance from them.

Julius read Roberta's mind and said "Don't worry, you have other attributes!"

Roberta jumped. "Sorry," she said. "I was thinking about what **Sappho** wrote about beauty: 'What is beautiful is good, and whoever is good will soon also be beautiful.' It seems that for Sappho the beautiful and the good are the same thing."

"We have already talked about that," Julius said. "For the Guides, beauty has the significance of an experience; a handsome man or a beautiful woman have very different experiences from the ones that normal men and women have, and for this reason the Guides deny that beauty is necessarily paired with goodness. True goodness is evolution and evolution transcends physicality, therefore beauty is only an experience that involves other experiences, such as being born male or female."

"When does one have the experience of beauty?" Roberta asked.

"When our consciousness creates the need for beauty. An individual who, for example, in an earlier incarnation has had the experience of ugliness, with everything that entails, needs the experience of beauty, which constitutes the other pole of the *duality* that regulates the evolution of the evolutive period called man. The Guides reason in a different way about beauty in an evolved individual. The medium Jesus, for example, who lent his body to the entity Christ so he could carry out his mission, needed a physical body structured in a certain way…"

"Why?" Roberta asked.

"So as to rivet the attention of the masses on him. The beauty of the man Jesus was an instrument of Christ's mission, just as the so-called miracles were."

"Then all the evolved beings ought to have an attractive body," Roberta said, without understanding the difference between the man Jesus and the entity Christ.

"It's not that way. The entity Christ was on a mission; the entity Christ is the *Lord of the World*. The Christ, who expressed himself through the body of the medium Jesus, is not only an evolved entity, *the Christ is evolution*. A completely different matter is the evolved being who lives the last reincarnation before leaving the cycle of rebirth behind; many of these evolved beings in the course of history have not needed an attractive physical body, because the nature of their life was not popular but mystic."

Roberta looked again at the woman sitting near them and perhaps attributed to her beauty a different meaning.

CEMETERIES

They took advantage of a call on a customer in Clivio dei Principi to visit the local monumental cemetery.

They entered through the main gate, where they were met by a wide avenue lined on both sides with the richest and most important tombs. They walked along among tall cypress trees, and Roberta was filled with a sense of greatness that soon she could not contain any longer. Almost without breathing she said "This place reminds me a lot of the **Foscolo**'s *Dei Sepolcri:*

> *The urns of the strong fire the strong soul*
> *to excelling deeds, O Pindemonte."*

"It is the usual suggestion resulting from the underlying illusion, which makes us believe that cemeteries have something to do with those who have passed on," Julius said. "The Guides never stop repeating, once again for the few insiders, that once the individual has left behind the *physical vehicle*, that vehicle returns to the *macrocosm that makes it up* and no longer has anything to do with the *feeling* that used it on the physical plane."

"Macrocosm...?" Roberta asked, not understanding.

"Yes, *macrocosm*: after the person passes on the various elements that make up our physical body, which the Guides call *microcosm*, decompose and return to the macrocosm, that is to say their state as elements, and become useful for other forms of life. It is the corpse that decays..."

"Why does our physical body have to return to being a thing after having lived for so long with us and for us?" Roberta asked.

"Because it has finished its task; it has been the *vehicle* of our experience on the physical plane and, after having fulfilled its function, it no longer has anything to do with us."

They stopped in front of a very fancy funerary chapel; inside they could see a large number of colour photo posters. The pictures were of the person who had died, a young man about twenty years old, photographed in various soccer moves. In the central picture the young man appeared wearing the jersey of a famous soccer team, holding a ball in one hand and a trophy in the other. "What would your Guides say about this show window?" Roberta said, standing by the door to the chapel, heavily covered with inlaid ivory.

"They would say that this is pure paganism, and whoever set up this temple of vacuous vanity shows that they still have a very elementary idea about death. They would add, however, that behaviour like this is the most evolved that the person who set up this expensive theatre could conceive."

"Why?" asked Roberta, even if by now she could guess the answer.

"Because whoever has such a primitive idea about death demonstrates that his consciousness is still insufficient. Even if – listen carefully – such a coarse idea about death is the right one for him, since it is the only one that will help him towards his subsequent evolution."

"According to your Guides, what idea did **Saint Augustine** have about death when he said: 'Those who have left us are not absent, they are invisible; they have their eyes full of glory on ours full of tears.' Would they agree?"

"They would agree on the concept that those who have passed on are not absent but invisible," Julius replied.

"Someone who passes on, in fact, simply moves his awareness first onto the astral plane and then onto the mental plane, which interpenetrate the physical plane. However, the Guides would not agree on the fact that all those who have passed on have their 'eyes full of glory'."

"Why?" Roberta asked.

"Because it is illusory to believe that someone who has passed on, for the very fact that he has passed on, abandons his degree of evolution and acquires another capable of making him live 'in glory'."

Old burial cells lined the sides of the cross-avenue of the cemetery. The first ones had been built on one level, but the later ones were mass-produced in sections up to five levels high.

Roberta reflected that that all those bodies represented existences that would never return again, and said bitterly "**Chateaubriand** in *Atala* left this saying: 'If a man returned to life some years after his death, I doubt he would be greeted with joy by the same people who grieved over his death.' Perhaps Chateaubriand was referring to the fact that a dead man's return would be a rupture in the natural order and could not help arousing unease even in those who loved him."

"I believe instead that the people who have such a definitive concept of death attribute to it a significance of total cancellation", Julius said, "which it is not."

They had stopped in a large open space, where the cemetery's most prestigious tombs towered high in competition with the cypresses. On the frontal of one was this Latin inscription: *Mors cuivis certa, nihil est invertius hora, ibimus absque mora, sed qua nescimus in ora*. Together they translated "Death is certain for all, but nothing is more uncertain than its hour; we shall leave without delay, but we do not know at what time."

"This inscription does not detract at all from the prevailing materialism," Julius said. "Indeed it is an exemplary case of pessimism. For the Guides, conversely, death is simply the passage of our awareness from a denser level of existence to one less dense."

"Try to translate that," Julius said, pointing to an inscription on the frontal of a smaller chapel.

Roberta read: '*Mortis vicinae vis vincet vim medicinae.*' She translated "The force of impending death will win out over the strength of medicine."

"Certainly," Julius said. "Because the moment of death is written and no science existing can delay it. It is the *individuality* that establishes the moment of death, not the *individual...*"

"What is the difference between *individuality* and *individual*?" Roberta asked.

"The *individual* is the *personality* you are, I am, in the *space-time* to which we are bound by our current incarnation. *Individuality*, conversely, is the *ensemble of all the personalities that we have experienced in our preceding incarnations and will experience in our following ones.* Then when, because of the evolution achieved, we no longer need to be reincarnated, we shall leave behind the cycle of birth and death. Therefore it is the *individuality* that marks the moment of death in the various incarnations, not the *individual*."

"I cannot seem to grasp properly the concept of *individuality*, and yet we have already talked about it," Roberta confessed.

"I'll use again the example the Guides give," Julius said. "We have seen that the tree's roots are the *spirit*; the *spirit* is the equivalent of the *individuality*. We have said that the trunk is the *consciousness* and the branches are the various *personalities* that the *individuality* assumes in its various incarnations, in the form of *individuals*. You and I are individuals. Therefore the *individuality*, since it is *spirit*, is the individual's true *divinity*, because it is at the same time the *Aleph Drop* and the *Tau Sensor* and encompasses also the *Principle*. Thus the branches of the tree, in other words the various *personalities* that the individual assumes in the various incarnations, are the *Logos* of that individual, that is to say *its manifestation in the worlds of perception and in the world of individual consciousness*."

"Sorry, I haven't really understood what personality is," Roberta said.

"Personality is the *filter* that every incarnate being has in front of consciousness, a filter that comes from egotism, from the I. In order to leave behind the cycle of rebirth, in other words to transcend the human condition, we have to constitute consciousness and to constitute consciousness we have to eliminate the *filters*, i.e., the ego."

"Now I think I understand", Roberta said, "but why do your Guides impart such a difficult teaching?"

"For two reasons: first, because this teaching is destined to posterity. Second, because, already now, each person understands it on his own level of evolution."

"You mean that each one has his level of reading the teaching?"

"Exactly. Each one has his level of understanding of the teaching, which is given to him, as always, by the breadth of his feeling."

"Can you give me an example?"

"Certainly. Many people manage to understand the truth of the teaching, for example, about reincarnation, but by experience I know that few succeed in understanding the truth of the *fusion* with all other beings, that is to say, the *fusion of the feeling.* This happens generally because the I *refuses to admit its extinction,* or to put it better, its being left behind."

"What does the I being left behind have to do with understanding?" Roberta said.

"It has everything to do with it, because the overcoming of the ego means evolution and thus understanding," Julius said.

They approached a little plaza filled with flowers, overlooked by hundreds of old burial cells. Many people were moving busily about them. All the cells were open and empty; the coffins had been taken out and placed in the middle of the plaza and opened. Next to the coffins were numerous urns, into which some workers, wearing grey smocks, were moving the remains they were taking out of the coffins.

When Roberta asked one of the workers what they were doing, he answered that thirty years after death, the law required them to move the remains into an urn.

They drew closer and saw that the workers were pulling pieces of bodies out of the open coffins and putting them into the urns. Some relatives of the deceased were watching the disinterment, but few coffins were attended by relatives; in many of them the workers grabbed the meagre remains and stuffed them into the urns.

Roberta and Julius saw in a coffin the body of an old lady dressed in black lace, while a worker shuffled through her bones. He picked out the ones still wrapped in a scrap of lace and then asked one of his co-workers into which urn he should put them. Each time, the co-worker answered that he didn't know, and the first man threw the lace-clad bones into just any urn.

"This way someone who has an urn with his loved one's name on it will think he has the loved one's remains, when in fact he'll have a mixture of remains and maybe none of them will belong to his loved one," Roberta observed.

"That's true," Julius said. "And it is right that it be this way, because the *physical body*, once it has been left behind, is only a *vehicle that is no longer in use*."

Then **Epictetus** is right," Roberta said, pulling some folded pieces of paper out of her pocket. "Listen to this:

> Being long occupied with the care of the body, that is to say personal exercise, eating, drinking, natural necessities, carnality, is a sign of a petty nature. These things should be done in passing, and all study should revolve around the mind."

"Perhaps Epictetus was right for the ancients", Julius said, "but now the Guides repeat that all study must revolve around consciousness, because it is time for man to *move his attention from the mind to consciousness*. It is time for a spiritual revolution, time for man not to draw his advancement from the illusion of outer life, but from his inner self, where the outer life begins."

"What about our body's *flaws*, of which **Saint Teresa of Avila** spoke – what would your Guides said about those? Listen to what Teresa says: 'Our body has this flaw, that the more care and comfort one pours on it the more it discovers necessities and needs'."

"They would comment in just one way," Julius said. "That our religious tradition is wrong in attributing an inferior significance to the body, as though it were a wild beast to be tamed. The right thing is to keep in balance, as the evolved being does, *all our bodies*: the higher bodies, astral, mental and akashic, but also the physical one, which has *equal dignity* with the other bodies."

"What do you mean by 'equal dignity'?" Roberta asked.

"That one must give the physical body the same importance given to the other bodies."

"Can you explain that better?"

"Take an intellectual, for example, who lives immersed in his *mental body*, for the most part ignoring the other bodies. This individual *does not have his bodies in balance*. So often the Law strikes him in the *physical terminal* of the body that the intellectual has favoured so exclusively…"

"Which is?" Roberta asked.

"The brain!"

"And how does it strike him?"

"Usually with a stroke."

"I had never thought of that," Roberta admitted. Through her mind ran the names of many famous intellectuals who had died that way.

"This is only an example," Julius added. "Nonetheless the Law has this tendency to strike the *body* that has been favoured much more than the others."

Meanwhile they had arrived in front of a magnificent chapel which overlooked a large open space, containing hundreds of graves in the ground. Roberta thought of a verse from the book of **Job**, 17:14: " I call the grave my father and the worm my mother or my sister." – Reciting the verse aloud,she said, "This is Job's cry against the suffering of the righteous."

"I would say against the suffering of the unrighteous", Julius corrected her, "because whoever suffers always deserves it, otherwise they would not suffer."

"The hard part about your Guides is that they never leave room for hope," Roberta said.

"On the contrary, we have repeated many times, the law of evolution, which is *perfect*, inexorably leads to Love, and for this reason leaves room only for hope, because Everything always and in any case works for the best. This means that someone who suffers could not avoid suffering, and even if he does not seem to be an unrighteous man, surely he was one and his suffering has to make him understand just this."

"What do you say about the line from Job?" Roberta asked, continuing not to understand the justice of pain.

"It is a line that is the distillation of a religious tradition, in which man is always seen as teetering on the border between life's misadventures, the endpoint of death, and punishment in the afterlife," Julius said. "The Guides give a completely different view of existence; for them, life is ongoing creation, evolution that reveals itself, also toil and pain, but always a step in the *evolutive equation* that leads the individual to transcend himself."

Roberta bent over double so she could read the headstone of a grave next to an ancient oak tree. She looked at the immense plant and said in awe "**Tagore** was right when he wrote: 'Trees are the boundless effort of the earth to talk to the listening sky'." She looked at Julius to seek his agreement.

"Trees are no different from the sky," Julius said instead. "In Reality, *macrocosm* and *microcosm* fuse together and the division between the lower earth that reaches towards the higher sky is completely illusory."

"In what sense do the macrocosm and microcosm fuse together?" Roberta asked.

"We have already talked about this. We are made up of *macrocosmic matter*," Julius said. "Our organs are composed of the same elements that make up the macrocosm, that is to say the planets, the earth, the mountains and the waters. Our body is made up of iron, calcium, phosphorus and many other elements, but at the same time we are also a *microcosm*…"

"This is what I can't understand: why are we also microcosm?"

"Because already the *mineral form* called *crystal* is inhabited by a primeval feeling, an *embryonic consciousness,* which makes the crystal the *first form of microcosmic life*."

"And then what happens?"

"It happens that the microcosm inhabits increasingly evolved forms of life, which traverse first the mineral and then the vegetable and animal kingdoms, until they come to man."

"Therefore we come from a crystal?"

"Yes, the first incarnational form of Being is the crystal. Not coincidentally, the Guides explain that the Earth's evolution goes *from the crystal to the saint.*"

"How is it possible that the crystal and saint are part of the same Being?" Roberta asked. "I don't see any relation between a crystal and a saint."

"Instead, a continuous relation exists. The individual begins his evolution on Earth in the most organized form of the mineral world, which is the *crystal* and which the Guides call *an atom of feeling*, and continues it in the vegetable, animal, and human worlds, up to the most evolved feeling that the human form can express, that is to say the feeling of the individual who loves others, because he has understood that others are himself. This is the feeling of the saint."

"And what does the saint *feel*? Roberta asked.

"He feels communion with all the creatures who are part of the All. He unveils the true reality of his Being, which is consciousness and thus communion with the All, which is macrocosm and microcosm together."

"Can you give an example?"

"Have you ever found yourself in front of a great show of nature, where the boundaries of your I trembled and for a few seconds fell down and you felt a blessedness you had never felt before?"

"Maybe that happened to me in Tanzania," Roberta said. "There everything was immense, the clouds, the trees, the termite nests as tall as little hills, to the sides of the enormous unpaved road…"

"What did you feel?"

"I was filled with that immensity…"

"As though your inner space had expanded enormously?"

"Yes, lost in that immensity…"

"Well, that *feeling* is a pale, pale, pale idea of what a Guide feels all the time."

"What made me feel that way?" Roberta asked.

"Everyone's whole life is a *vibratory event* scattered among the various bodies. The Guides call these events *codes*, which reign both in the *microcosm*, that is to say in living creatures, and in the macrocosm, in what we call *things* and also in the macrocosmic aspect of living creatures.

"The *macrocosmic aspect* of living beings is our *physical body.* Indeed, in Reality – we should reiterate this – the microcosm and macrocosm are not separate, and in fact after death, the elements that make up the physical vehicle which the microcosm has used go back to being the macrocosm."

"I'm having a hard time following you," Roberta said.

"I mean that when our body has become a corpse, the various elements that make up our physical body: iron, phosphorus, potassium, etc., return to the *macrocosmic life* because they are no longer needed by the vehicle that on the physical plane was useful for the experience of the individual, i.e. the microcosm."

"Maybe we have already talked about this," Roberta said.

"Sorry, I'm repeating myself", Julius admitted, "because the teaching is a *comprehensive structure,* whose parts refer always to the other parts, which in turn serve to explain the overall structure. Now, to make you forgive me, I want to talk to you about a topic I have never mentioned, and that is the mistake we make in the customs that accompany the moment of passing on."

"Mistakes?" Roberta said.

"Yes, mistakes, which could be called *technical* because they get in the way of the laws that regulate the decomposition of bodies. Westerners commonly believe, for example, that the colour black repels the negativity of the event. For the Guides, though, it is a mistake to wear dark colours when one is in mourning, and above all it is a mistake to stay in the room where the body has been laid out while dressed in dark colours. As happens with light, which is attracted by black instead of being repelled by it, so it is for the *elemental spirits* that, when the physical body has been left behind by the consciousness and the ethereal parts of the principal organs begin to detach, start working on the decomposition of the body."

"What happens?"

"It happens that these *elemental spirits* have no powers of discernment and are attracted wherever they find sources from which they draw energy, and thus from the *bodies dressed in dark colours*. Therefore it is detrimental to remain in the room with the deceased wearing mourning, since much of the sense of oppression that one feels in front of a corpse comes right from the activity of the *elemental spirits* that are working not only on the corpse that has to be decomposed but *also on the people wearing black*. It is very helpful, instead, to wear soft colours and maybe watch over the deceased for the night after his death, not the following night or afterwards."

"Why should the colours be soft?"

"Because the *elemental spirits* are not attracted to them. A light colour would be better and best of all would be white, if we did not consider it blasphemous for mourning."

"Why is a wake helpful?"

"Because abandoning the body to itself can cause deep fears in the person who has passed on. It is as though we felt defrauded of something of ours that remains at the mercy of just anybody. Moreover, the deceased who is in a *medium* state of evolution remains tied to the place where his body is laid and to the body itself. The wake, if performed by people who are dear to him, enables the deceased to feel reassured and to move away more quickly from the place where his body is laid."

"Why should the wake not last more than one night after the death?"

"Because only after the first night following death does the entity with *medium evolution* manage to move away from his body. And he does not succeed in doing this easily if he still sees his loved ones around him. Of course, I am talking about a *moving away of the consciousness*."

"Do you know what the wisdom of your Guides makes me think of?" Roberta said when they were once again near the massive cemetery gates.

"Man's ignorance," Julius hazarded a guess.

"No, an immense desire for freedom, for not needing this wisdom any more, which can become a fetter. Maybe it is the same desire for freedom of which **Aurobindo** spoke when he said: 'The whole world yearns after freedom, yet each creature is in love with his chains; this is the first paradox and inextricable knot of our nature'."

"I instead am certain that every creature loves his chains, until his evolution enables him to unfasten them and to move on to less heavy ones", Julius said, "and so on until he leaves the wheel of incarnations behind. Under this aspect, what Aurobindo says and what you *feel* in his words is a *truth that is a point of passage*."

"Truth that is a point of passage?" Roberta asked.

"Yes, the *truth that is a point of passage* is a step of understanding higher than the preceding step and lower than the next one. It is a truth that was useful but has to be transcended. Furthermore, the Guides would not agree with Aurobindo when he speaks of an *inextricable knot of our nature,* because for them there are no knots that evolution cannot extricate."

They were in the plaza in front of the cemetery and made their way through the dazzle of cars parked in the sun. Roberts said, "Then **Confucius** was right when he said: 'The superior man is like an archer: if he misses the target, he looks for the reason in himself'."

"If by *superior man* Confucius means someone who no longer belongs to the band of *medium evolution* but to the *middle-upper* one, then that is right. He alone has reached a feeling like that."

They threaded their way for a while among the scorching-hot cars and came to theirs.

All that effort made Roberta think of what **Rajneesh** said in the *Book of Secrets*: "Life is one movement, and the moment you define you create a mess, because definitions will be dead, and life is an alive movement."

"Very nice line", Julius said, "but the masters would add, yes, *life is one movement,* but it is inner movement."

"Which means?" said Roberta.

"Imagine you are looking at a strip of film against the light, frame after frame. Now imagine that this film strip is life and you looking at the film are the one who is living it. In reality, what moves?"

"Nothing."

"That's right, *only your inner being moves,* as it lives every frame it has sensations, emotions, desires, thoughts, that *feel* the film, frame after frame."

"Thus this line from Rajneesh that life is an alive movement, your Guides would replace it by saying that life is an inner movement," Roberta concluded, climbing into the car.

"That's exactly right," Julius confirmed.

They came out of the cemetery parking lot and immediately had to deal with the traffic. In the stifling heat of the car, Roberta asked again "On the subject of Eastern wisdom, what would your Guides say about this thought from **Ramakrishna**? – 'Disease is the tax which the soul pays for the body, as the tenant pays house-rent for the use of the house'."

"They would say that disease is not a 'tax' but an evolutive necessity, thus an opportunity to understand which the Law gives the individual."

"Is disease a necessity or an opportunity?" Roberta asked.

"It is a *necessity* that the Law forces on the individual when there is no other way to make him evolve. At the same time, disease is an *opportunity* that the Law gives the individual so that he can draw *evolutive essence* from it. It depends on the individual."

"What if the individual does not understand?"

"Then the Law, which is *impersonal* and never tires, presents him with similar illnesses, similar situations, similar vibratory events, similar film frames, similar experiences, similar ways of living, similar forms of life. All these terms are synonyms for the Guides," Julius said.

The traffic moved slowly and Roberta remembered that they had come to Clivio dei Principi to call on a customer. They drew up next to an elderly woman to ask information about the road to take, and the woman answered very graciously.

When they were on their way once again, Roberta asked "What do your Guides say about the 'golden years'?"

"What most people do not even imagine", Julius answered, "and that is that old age is the *supernormal period* of human life, that is to say life's most spiritual period, which comes after youth which is the *instinctive period* and adulthood, which is the *intellectual period*."

"What about you, how are you living your *supernormal period*", Roberta smiled, "since you are already 60?"

"I am not living it as well as I could", Julius replied, "because I have a too intellectual, too *dual* view of the teaching."

In reality, *duality* divided his life, and yet their relationship was not just based on work and spiritual seeking. Julius had insisted on accompanying Roberta to the hospital on the day she had to undergo a gastroscopy. The procedure consisted of introducing an endoscope first into her mouth and then down the oesophagus as far as the stomach. A tiny video camera on the tip of the endoscope would reveal what was causing Roberta's frequent digestive problems. Julius had accompanied her because the procedure caused a strong vomiting reflex and sense of suffocation. Roberta had insisted in vain that she could go alone. Julius had said to her "Aren't you and I one?" They reached the hospital and waited their turn.

They remained silent in front of the suffering crowd until, even there, Roberta shot another arrow from the quiver of her memory. "In my opinion", she said, "**Nicolas de Chamfort** is right when he says in *Maxims and Thoughts*: 'When one considers the way the sick are treated in hospitals, one would say that human beings have thought of these sad asylums, not to take care of the sick, but to keep the sight of them away from the happy people whose joys would be troubled by these sufferers'."

"It depends on the observation point you are using," Julius said. "The Guides would not approve of this thought, because for them happiness is a *temporary state of consciousness*, as long as one is living the human condition. Therefore, in the great majority of cases, a real distinction between happy and unhappy is illusory."

"Do your Guides not make a distinction even between the healthy and the sick?" Robert asked sceptically.

"The distinction is a feeble one because health and sickness are also states of consciousness and depend on how the healthy and the ill live them. It is no coincidence that many people who kill themselves not only enjoy good health but often have everything."

The clinic looked like a bivouac. The waiting crowd was crossed by another crowd that the nurses called into the rooms. People mingled and rushed to grab the seats that had been left free, settling down into their meek waiting.

"These people remind me of something **Marcuse** said in *Eros and Civilization*," Roberta said. "The individual lives the universal destiny of the species. The past determines the present, since mankind has not yet succeeded in dominating its own history."

"What does that mean, 'mankind has not yet succeeded in dominating its own history'?" Julius asked.

"Maybe Marcuse meant that history eludes mankind because it is always something worse than the mankind that is living it," Roberta guessed.

"For the Guides, this interpretation would be absurd", Julius said, "because history expresses mankind's evolutive needs and is thus the *true reflection* of the mankind that is living it."

"What does it mean that history is the true reflection of the mankind that is living it?"

"That every historical event is created by the *consciousness form* of the mankind living that event. This means that history is not something *outside* those who lived before us, or outside us or our posterity. It is produced by our evolutive needs projected onto the mirror of life in the form of collective and individual experiences."

"Why do you call it 'consciousness form'?"

"Because it is the *physical form* that the collective consciousness *demands* to assume. For the collectivity, the *physical form* is represented by the events that we call *historical* while for single individuals the *physical form* is represented by their lives."

Like a gust of wind, a nurse threw open the door to the room and shouted Roberta's last name. She stood up and walked through the crowd. The nurse asked her if she had anyone to stay with her during the procedure and Julius was called in. They waited a while longer.

Roberta thought of two lines from *Gerusalemme Liberata*:

The fear of ill is a worse ill,
Perhaps, than the present ill would seem.

"**Tasso** is right," Julius agreed. "We have to live only in the present, excluding from our life the past and the future."

"Why?" Roberta asked.

"We have already talked about this. Because in a Reality that has no time except evolutive time, the past is what makes us be what we are and the future is what we are preparing to be. Therefore we should be interested only in this moment, the *here and now,* in a word, the present," Julius said.

Roberta was about to fire off another question when they were called in for the procedure. The nurse had her lie down on a table on her side and told Julius to stand at the head of the table. Then they were forgotten once again.

Roberta asked the question "**Juvenal** in his *Satires* says: '*Orandum est ut sit mens sana in corpore sana.*' – Pray to have a healthy mind in a healthy body. So then, if I do not have a healthy body, does this mean I don't have a healthy mind?"

"I believe that Juvenal, instead of 'mind,' should have said 'consciousness'," Julius said.

"Then it is the consciousness that protects us from illness?"

"Not the consciousness but the *constituted consciousness* protects us from illness. It is true that the mind controls the body but it is also true that the mind *takes orders* from the consciousness, and thus it is the consciousness that – in the last analysis – has to be healthy: that is to say, *constituted*. Instead, for prayer that can be made with the mind or the consciousness, the Guides say something else. Do you remember another great who talked about prayer?" Julius asked.

"Yes, **Kafka**, who says in the *Diaries*, 'Write like a form of prayer.' Why did you ask me that?"

"Because I am intrigued by the difference between prayer as 'laymen', like Juvenal and Kafka, understand it and as the Guides understand it. They give it a completely different meaning. For the Guides, prayer is such not when one pleads one's own case, but when one pleads the case of others, in other words when prayer is an altruistic thought."

"Can you give an example?" Roberta said, shifting a little from the position in which they had put her.

"**The Lord's Prayer**, for example, is a totally altruistic prayer, and it is no coincidence that it was dictated by Christ. It never says 'give me' but 'give us,' it never refers to an I or a mine but always to an 'us,' which represents Reality."

Finally a tall, heavyset doctor rushed in, clutching the endoscopy machine like a pile of books. He confirmed

Roberta's name, had her lie down in the exact position, and threaded into her mouth a flexible tube that he pushed farther and farther down. Roberta first felt the discomfort of a foreign body in her throat and then a growing sense of suffocation which filled her eyes with tears. Julius put his hand on her shoulder. The doctor pushed the tube farther down and ordered, "Don't cough, breathe!"

Long seconds passed when it seemed like she had no more breath. When the tube reached her stomach the doctor moved his eyes close to a viewer and began his diagnosis – "Multiple superficial erosions at the third distal of the oesophagus. What kind of disposition do you have?" he asked.

Roberta could not answer because she was overcome with a sense of suffocation. And yet the words of **Shu** in *The Book of the Cynic* popped into her head:

"The worst of men always receive praise,
at the end of their lives, engraved on their tombstone."

She felt Julius's hand on her shoulder, but could not ask him what the Guides would have said about this line. So she tried to answer the question by herself, in light of what she had learned from the teaching. The answer came to her easily – there are no worst of men but only individuals in the process of evolution and, quite rightly, tombstones always speak well of the dead because each one acts as well as is permitted to him by his degree of evolution.

Roberta was pleased with her answer and thought it would be worthy of Julius. At that moment, the doctor moved the tube and Roberta felt suffocated once again.

"The cardia is gaping", said the doctor, "but there is no evidence of gastroesophageal prolapse."

"What do you mean by gaping?" Julius asked.

"That it remains wide open."

Overwhelmed by the endoscope, Roberta listened in a half stupor. She thought of **Bacon**'s words in his essay *On Adversity* – 'Prosperity is the blessing of the Old Testament; adversity is the blessing of the New.' She did not know how to interpret the thought, but she took advantage of the breaths her vomiting reflex permitted her to take to think. "What use is a close study of the Scriptures if the Guides say that the Scriptures are in large part symbolic or made up by men?"

She remembered the Julius had told her many times that the Scriptures, in any case, contain the essential part of Christ's teaching and that the Gospel of John is the least made-up of the Scriptures because it had undergone the least manipulation. She was satisfied with this answer and thought that in the future she too would be capable of evaluating the thought of the Greats in light of the Guides' teaching.

"The gastric mucus is diffusely hyperaemic, such as in a flare-up of chronic gastritis," the doctor said hurriedly. "All we need to do now is get a nice sample for the Helicobacter Pylori test and we'll be done."

Roberta was once again racked with heaves and once again felt Julius's warm hand on her shoulder. She thought then that Julius was getting to be a habit with her and she remembered a line from **Pliny the Elder** in his *Natural History*: "Habit is in all things the best teacher." She asked herself, "Is Julius a teacher for me?"

She thought so, and continued to herself, "It is true, Julius has shown me a new way of looking at people and life."

"The pylorus is normal," the doctor affirmed. "But the duodenal bulb has points of inflammation, as in duodenitis."

"Are you a worrier?" he asked.

"Pretty much," Julius answered in Roberta's place.

"The ampulla of Vater is normal," the doctor concluded. He pulled the endoscope out of her throat, and Roberta felt like herself again, but she immediately felt the burning sensation of her mucous membranes irritated by the passage of the tube. She remained gasping on the table.

Julius patted her on the shoulder. "Come on, it's all over!" he said, and they exchanged an affectionate glance.

Roberta's trachea was still on fire when they came out of the hospital and walked towards the parking lot. Here they had an unpleasant surprise: someone had parked his car across theirs and was blocking them from backing out.

They waited a few minutes. Then **Flaubert**'s entry for imbeciles in his *Dictionary of Received Ideas* popped into her mind: "Imbeciles: those who do not think like we do."

"In your opinion, is the person who blocked our car an imbecile or just someone who does not think like we do?" she said.

"Neither one nor the other," Julius answered. "He is only another of us who right now is the *mirror of our limitation,* otherwise we would not have *created-perceived* him."

"Do you mean that we ourselves created somebody to keep us from getting out of the parking lot?" Roberta asked.

"Certainly. This is why the Guides repeat that our life is a series of experiences; that is to say of *mirrors*, where we reflect our *limitations* in the form of *persons* we meet and *situations* we live."

"I don't get it..."

"Do you remember the example of the ocean? The Guides explain that everything that happens to a drop happens to the ocean, which in turn reflects the drop's reaction. And what makes us still perceive drops, that is to say *individuals*, is our relative view of Reality, a view imposed on us by our still insufficient evolution..."

They continued talking for a long time, without being able to get out of the parking lot, until the owner of the car that was blocking them arrived. He did not favour them even with a glance and slid behind the steering wheel without apologizing. He took his time pulling out. Julius got out of the car and walked over to the man. He asked him to roll down the window and said to him "You took possession of almost an hour of our life because you prevented us from leaving the parking lot. Don't you have anything to say?"

"It has happened to me lots of times," the man said scruffily.

"I have never blocked anybody," Julius said.

"Then you've been wrong, because in life sometimes you give and sometimes you take," the man shot back.

"No, I've been right", Julius said, "if this has helped me not to live like you…"

"What do you mean?" asked the man, stopping his car in the middle of the parking lot.

"I mean that you are still unaware of the fact that other people exist!"

The man snickered without understanding, put his car in gear and drove off, tyres squealing. Julius joined Roberta in the car and manoeuvred to get out of the parking lot. Even with her throat on fire, Roberta managed to ask "Why did you lecture that man when he didn't understand a thing?"

"Because you should always express your opinions, never imposing them but proposing them. It is up to the listener to take them into consideration or not."

"But he was an ass," Roberta said.

"When he is less of an ass, maybe what he heard today will help him evolve. Meanwhile I have planted my opinion, like a seed, in his unconscious."

"You put too much importance on opinions," Roberta said. "*In his Essay on the Immediate Data of Consciousness*, **Bergson** says: 'The opinions we care about the most are the ones we would find hardest to explain, and the very reasons we use to justify them are rarely the same ones that led us to adopt them.' It seems that for Bergson opinions are highly meretricious."

"For the Guides too, opinions, as an exclusive product of the mind, have very little importance, because the mind is illusion. Nonetheless, opinions can be inspired in the mind by the consciousness, and in this case they are important, because they report the individual's evolution..."

Roberta braked suddenly and Julius stopped talking. A short distance from them a beautiful woman was walking practically in the middle of the street, as though to make people look at her. Roberta cleared her aching throat and commented, "See, a woman like that fascinates even me!"

The woman crossed the street in front of them. Her slender ankles and taut legs made her a high-class woman. Her pointed breasts drew attention to her. She had a haughty walk, and she looked in every way like an object of desire.

"A woman like that stirs up even my old hormones," Julius admitted. "Maybe she is a top model."

"For you, then, **Freud** is wrong," Roberta said, "when in *Civilization and its Discontents* he says: 'The sexual life of civilized man is severely compromised; it sometimes gives the impression of being a function in regression, as seems to be the case with certain of our organs like teeth or hair'."

"For the Guides, Freud was right for his times", Julius said, "because his doctrine is based entirely on the mind and one could say that it is the triumph of the mind. Suffice it to think of the importance Freud gives sex stripped of any consciousness, sex which is instead a sublime instrument for union with another and thus, with Absolute Being. It is no coincidence that the Guides explain that one of the countless ways to immerse oneself in the *state of consciousness called God* is the one that ancient esotericism called *via sexualis*."

"Do you mean t*he path of sex?*"

"Yes, but sex understood as the *physical completion of a state of consciousness that yearns for union*; thus the *path* that leads to both spiritual and physical *fusion* with another being."

"Then sex, in its real essence, is almost unknown," Roberta admitted.

"It is unknown in medium evolution, because people in this phase live sex in an uninvolved way. Who is capable, for example, of understanding that orgasm is a very pale reflection of the beatitude that one lives constantly on the plane of consciousness?"

"Is this why some saints reach an orgasm during ecstasy?" Roberta asked.

"Certainly. The Guides explain that ecstasy, or Samadhi, as ecstasy is called in the Eastern world, is the *momentary perception of the akashic plane or consciousness,* in which the awareness of the incarnate individual is influenced by its part of Akasha. It is a perception that is translated into an *ineffable spiritual beatitude* that resonates in the physical body as *orgasm.*"

"When you speak of beatitude, it reminds me of **Vivekananda**, when he says in *Raja Yoga*, 'The first sign that one is becoming religious is that one becomes joyous.' For you, does the teaching of the Guides, which is your religion, make you joyous?"

"Two objections," Julius said. "The first is that if one believes the teaching of the Guides, one cannot adhere to any religion, because they proclaim the *religion of innerness* and thus one would fall into an irresolvable contradiction. The second is that perhaps I would be cheerful if I *were* the teaching and I did not limit myself to knowing the teaching – but this is not my case because I still think about the teaching, I don't *feel* it."

"When does one feel the teaching?" Roberta bleated the question out, because her throat was killing her.

"We have talked about this many times," Julius said. "*Feeling* the teaching means living it in consciousness, as an evolved being lives it. To talk about a Western evolved being of recent times who is well-known, the Guides cite the example of Padre Pio. In effect, the *evolutive period called Padre Pio* was very ignorant. The Latin formulas he repeated all his life were in large part erroneous, and yet that man *was the teaching* because he *was the union* with the All, of which the Guides speak. And the paranormal events in which he was involved demonstrate how much he was in union with the *higher planes of being*."

"Did the paranormal events depend on the quality of the religion to which Padre Pio belonged?" Roberta asked.

"They depended exclusively on his degree of evolution which, being a state of consciousness, did not need any religious nameplate, any human label. Padre Pio spoke of the devils that inflicted tremendous temptations on him at night, but those were hallucinations which came to him from his *mental body*, from his extreme religious convictions. The *lower bodies,* that is to say the physical, astral and mental bodies, are one thing and the consciousness, which is the true seat of individual evolution, is another."

"So one can be a protagonist of the same paranormal phenomena produced by Padre Pio without belonging to any religion?" Roberta asked.

"Without belonging to any organization whether religious or secular," Julius confirmed. He then added, "When I was younger, I knew a man who had a family and children and was a sales representative for Goodyear, the American tyre company. He was a good man, and he had always pursued the ideal of the life of Christ and was known for his goodness not only in the neighbourhood and his workplace, but also the places where he did an immense amount of volunteer work. One day, while he was on his way to call on a customer at Baucche Basse, he felt a strange sense of discomfort and was forced to stop his car at a fountain in the middle of the open country. He put his wrists under the water to cool off and realized that the water was turning red. He opened his hands and saw that on each palm there was a little wound that was bleeding. Those were and remained his stigmata."

"And nobody ever knew about this?" Roberta asked.

"Very few, because behind this Goodyear sales rep there was no organization like the Church to take over an event that gave it prestige. As you see, there are also secular stigmata and they are produced, just like the religious ones, by a state of consciousness that sets in motion a phenomenon called 'ideoplasia'. Therefore it is easy to understand that a state of consciousness has no need of anything else to produce its effects."

"Then **Bakunin** was right", Roberta said, "when he wrote in the *Program of the International Brotherhood*: 'Every political and social organization is founded on the negation or at least a restriction of the absolute principle of liberty and must necessarily arrive at iniquity or disorder'."

"Maybe Bakunin had intuited the *collective I*, and thus the *state of consciousness called collective egois* which is lurking behind every organization", Julius said, "and as a good anarchist he gave this insight a destructive charge. But the Guides repeat that there is no need to destroy the organizations that are outside us, which instead are useful for those who still believe in organizations, but it is our inner being that has to be organized, because evolution happens only inside us."

"In what way?" Roberta asked again.

"To be precise: by not delegating our evolution to any organization, not adhering to any religion, esoteric school, sect, or ideology, not idolatrizing any Western, Eastern, yoga, martial arts, art, ideological, or political teacher, not taking part in any pilgrimages whether lasting two hours, a day, a month, a year; not fleeing in search of peace in distant lands, because our best is already in us. These are all escapes that take us farther away from our true goal, which is our inner self."

Meanwhile they had reached Julius's house. He got out of the car and thought that Roberta was about to leave alone and in pain, so he invited her in for dinner.

"Certainly, the human soul is boundless," Roberta said as they climbed the stairs. "You never know where it starts and where it ends. Or perhaps does one have to distinguish between one soul and another, as the Chinese poet **Ch'en Chiu** said? 'It is hard to know a man. But a man who is easy to know is perhaps not worth the trouble'."

"It is not just hard," Julius said. "If it is a man who wants to know another man, it is actually even impossible. For the Guides maintain, a man can be known only by someone who is no longer a man and has transcended the human condition. Moreover, it is illusory to create a hierarchy between men who are easy or are hard to get to know, because each of us, during our various incarnations, has been easy or difficult countless times, according to the personality in which our being was wrapped."

They were on the porch of Julius's little apartment. He turned the key and they went in. Julius cast a fond glance over the room he used as his entrance, lined with books and tapes.

Once again Roberta noticed how much her friend loved this place and said "I'll bet that right now, you would not agree with **Proudhon**, when he wrote: *'La proprieté c'est le vol.'* – Property is theft."

Julius walked around the large plywood table that took up most of the room and went to sit down on the other side of the table, in a large high-backed chair.

"In effect", he said, "if we were more evolved, property would no longer exist, but since we are not yet that way, we must use property as a means for personal evolution."

"In what way?" Roberta asked.

"In the only way possible, by using property altruistically."

Roberta sat on the big plywood table, which bent dangerously under her weight.

"Watch out!" Julius said. "This is a virtual table." Then he explained that he had had the table made in order to accommodate the participants in the group gatherings he held at his house. "The chair I am sitting in is the one where the instrument sits," he said.

"Who is the instrument?" Roberta asked.

"Some Guides call *instrument* what was once called a medium. It is a definition in line with the progress of the phenomenon and, to my mind, is more up-to-date than the term medium. In fact, to communicate with the physical plane, the Guides use the physical body of an incarnate being, which acts as an instrument, hence the term. What is more, some *instruments* now receive also messages from our 'space brothers', which others sometimes call 'aliens', 'extraterrestrials', or 'UFOs'."

Roberta looked at the large plywood table which overwhelmed the room. The table legs were thin and showed that its construction was amateurish.

"Who made this table?" she asked.

"An old carpenter, who did not charge me very much. Sometimes we have twenty or thirty people at our gatherings, and they need somewhere to put their tape recorders and read the questions they ask the Guides. The table can be dismantled, but since it was put here I've never taken it down."

"Why?" Roberta asked.

"Because the meetings with the Guides are my life, and it is no use depriving myself of a symbol of this love, even if it takes up almost my whole house."

"Then you would not agree with **Jalal al-Din Rumi**, when he said: 'Do not bind your heart to any dwelling, because you will suffer when they take it away from you'."

"Of course I do not agree, even if I should – because by now I know that the true dwelling-place is the inner being, – the *heart* is, in the romantic sense, the place where the rite of individual evolution is celebrated."

Then Julius caressed the large tape recorder which reigned over the table and looked at Roberta. "How many hours have I spent next to this chair", he said, "where the instrument sits in a trance, while red lights of the tape recorder blink on and off according to the volume of his voice. On Saturdays, the Guides impart the teaching to the entire group, and those are the canonical meetings; then on Thursdays we are alone, the instrument and I, in front of the recorder during the work session."

"Work?" Roberta asked.

"Yes, the Thursday séance is devoted entirely to the questions I ask the Guides."

"What kind of questions?"

"All kinds. The answers the Guides give on Thursday contain a large part of the lesser teachings which I use when we comment on the thoughts of the greats, which you constantly set forth. Then, starting on Friday, I transcribe the tapes."

"Transcribe?" Roberta asked once again.

"Yes, I put the transcription of the tapes on to the computer. It is a job that takes a long time, because every week I have two or three 90-minute tapes to transcribe."

"Can you give me an example of the questions you ask the Guides on Thursdays?"

"They concern daily life. When I think of a question that I consider interesting, wherever I am, I make note of it so as not to forget it. Then I read it during the séance."

Roberta wandered a little around the table; she was thinking that Julius had truly made mediumship his life. At his age, a man living alone, with an exhausting job like sales representative, spent his free time listening to the voices of Guides that, according to him, came from the higher planes of existence; voices that, still according to him, were *consciousness*. And yet Roberta was very fond of Julius, not so much for what he believed as for the faith he showed. It was the faith Julius had in the Guides that made her fond of him, a faith that attracted without lures or flattery, simply by the strength of its existence.

Roberta admitted "What especially attracts me in what you are saying is how you say it, how you present it. Have you ever thought that you could have this effect on others?"

"The Guides have an explanation for this, too", Julius replied, "because they explain that whoever has a faith, whatever it is, by the very fact of living in the *monoideism* that every faith entails, has first created and then energized a very powerful thought form…"

"Monoideism…?" Roberta said.

"Yes, monoideism is thinking essentially of one sole idea; in my case, the Guides' teaching. The *thought form* created by *monoideism* can be likened to a *magnetic train* that attracts all those who have *cognate,* or *similar codes* to the *thought form* which that faith energizes."

"Can you give an example?"

"Certainly. You, for example, have *similar codes* to the *thought form* in which I too am inserted, otherwise you would not be here. This happens because everything is vibration, everything is *code in the universe.* Intuiting this reality is difficult, and it is no coincidence that the Guides explain that understanding the unicity of universal manifestations is the ultimate goal the human mind can conceive."

MEMORIES

A song down below…
It is a beggar.
If he sings, this old ma
Who possessed nothing,
Why do you weep
You, who have such nice memories?

"What do you think of that?" Roberta asked. "**Du Fu** is an ancient Chinese poet whose work decreed the triumph of classicism."

Julius shook himself out of his lethargy and realized he was in the car. In a relatively short time, he remembered that they were going to call on an important customer, who might buy a number of industrial washing machines.

"Why did you think of Du Fu?" he asked.

"Because the immigrant who wanted to clean our windshield at the stoplight was singing."

Julius asked Roberta to repeat Du Fu's lines, and then said "The state of consciousness in which one operates has nothing to do with social rank. An experience like poverty can be lived in a different way by each person who lives it because *each one's codes* are different. Then, Du Fu speaks of memories. Memories are the revisiting of experiences that have already produced their *evolutive essence*. Therefore from the standpoint of the new evolution we have to attain, living in memories, no matter how sweet, is completely useless and, in fact, highly *crystallizing* because it produces *evolutive stagnation*. And stagnation attracts pain, which the Law uses to break apart the crystallization of the individual."

They were driving past long rows of election posters which had not yet been taken down. On all sides, campaign slogans called attention to a party. Like an echo, **Nehru**'s words resounded in Roberta's mind: "Democracy and socialism are means to an end, not ends in themselves."

"What do you think of that?" she asked while the billboards disappeared into the darkness of the outskirts of the city.

"That's the way it is," Julius answered. "There is no political formula, ideology, individual or collective experience that is an end in itself, but everything happens for one sole purpose, to produce evolution in the individual and in the collectivity. Then, when everything has served its purpose, it ceases to exist to make way for the *religion of consciousness* which each person will celebrate in his inner being."

"Then what would your Guides say about **Marx**'s famous line – 'Religion is the opiate of the masses'? This line was then taken up by Lenin and became the slogan of the Communist fight against religious influence."

"They would certainly say that Marx, as a good materialist, had not perceived that the physical plane is under the dominion of spiritual causes; that everything that happens has a higher meaning. Religions have been and will be useful as long as they are of service. And when will they be transcended? When people no longer need them and evolution has liberated mankind from slavery; when it is understood that religions are not the exclusive concessionaries for the world beyond. They will remain the *opiate of the masses* as long as the masses need their opiate, but these will be fewer and fewer."

They drove along the walls of the ancient Felice aqueduct, where large caverns perforated the stones, inhabited by gypsies and tramps. Rarely did the outskirts of a big city demonstrate such an advanced state of urban decay.

They came on to the provincial road, where the aqueduct stretched in a long straight line, where enormous graffiti murals exploded towards the sky with ferocious images. Some showed a movie hero pointing his machine gun at everybody.

Roberta pulled up by the side of the road and, opening her agenda, pulled out a handwritten note and said "Listen to this thought by **Shen Tsung-chi'en** on painting. I added it to my collection just yesterday:

> *Those who have curried the innocence of the spirit*
> *must not paint.*
> *Those who love luxury must not paint.*
> *Those who fight for power and money*
> *must not paint.*
> *Those whose minds are full of low and shameful*
> *thoughts must not paint.*
> *All of them, swept up in the whirlwind of the world*
> *and fashion, have nothing to do with refinement*
> *and elegance of spirit.*

What do you think?"

"I think that everyone has to try everything, not only painting. Lifting one human activity above the others is a mistake. What the Guides say can seem absurd for someone who observes his neighbour within the sphere of just one incarnation, but it becomes Reality if it is viewed within the sphere of multiple incarnations."

"I have not understood how many incarnations each of us has," Roberta said.

"We have already spoken of the three groups of incarnations, *instinctive, intellectual,* and *supernormal,*" Julius said.

"You spoke of it when the sales director was promoted", Roberta recalled, "and then I found out they thought you were crazy."

"That has often happened to me, but the Guides repeat 'Answer those who ask you,' and that is what I do. If then they think I'm crazy, in any case I have done what I think is right."

"There was that tall clerk in the Personnel Office", Roberta remembered, "who said that mediumship is condemned by the Church..."

"Once upon a time," Julius confirmed. "But now the Church, also through the words of theologians, states that contact with those who have gone on before is possible."

This time it was Julius who took a slip of paper out of his wallet and read it.

"The books of the Old Testament", he said, "speak of calling up spirits in the episode involving King Saul, the witch of Endor, and the spirit of Samuel (I Samuel 28:7-11). Because of its importance, this episode deserves mention and this is why I always carry the passage with me."

"The Old Testament?" Roberta said.

"Yes, it is unimpeachable testimony. 'Endor' means 'spring of Dor' and was a village that belonged to the tribe of Manasseh, where a woman lived who practiced necromancy. Saul went to her to ask her about his future and to call up the spirit of Samuel. I'll read you the passage: 'So he said to his servants, 'Find me a woman who has a familiar spirit, and I will go and inquire through her.' His servants told him there was such a woman at En-dor... The woman asked whom she should call up, and Saul answered, Samuel'."

"I did not know there was such a precise confirmation of mediumship in the Old Testament," Roberta commented.

"On the contrary, it exists, even if many pretend not to see it. Nonetheless, the Guides repeat that accepting or not the contact with the *higher planes of existence* is not a question of proof or permission from the Church, but of *feeling*. This means that, even with the testimony of the Old Testament, believing in mediumship is an extremely personal experience.

"To get back to your question about the number of incarnations, we should reiterate that there exist three bands of human incarnations, which the Guides call *instinctual, intellectual* and *supernormal* incarnations. These three incarnational bands serve to transcend the *three groups of limitations* that are called in turn *instinctual, intellectual,* and *supernormal limitations*. Therefore, the *instinctual limitations* are transcended in the *band of instinctual incarnations,* the *intellectual limitations* in the *band of intellectual incarnations,* and the *supernormal limitations* in the *band of supernormal incarnations*. Each band of incarnations is made up of about a hundred incarnations, which is why the Guides state that human incarnations number 343, that is 49 x 7..."

"Wait a minute!" Roberta said. "What good does it do to know all this stuff?"

"It does us little or no good," Julius admitted. "It serves for posterity. This is why the Guides, starting right now, hand down – together with the moral teaching – this teaching that can be called esoteric."

"Why do they divide the incarnations into 49 x 7?"

"Because 7 is the number of *shells* that make up an individual's akashic body or consciousness. And while the physical, astral, and mental vehicles were formed during the evolution acquired in the preceding natural reigns, which are the mineral, vegetable, and animal kingdoms, the *akashic vehicle or consciousness* is made up *shell by shell,* seven incarnations by seven incarnations, from the moment when an individual begins to evolve as a man."

"Why seven by seven incarnations?"

Because each shell in turn is made up of seven *subshells,* which represent seven *limitations,* and it takes an average of seven incarnations to overcome one limitation completely. Thus, to make up a complete shell of the akashic vehicle or consciousness of an individual, it will take 7 x 7, or 49 incarnations. Then, the period of *instinctual incarnations* will comprise *two akashic shells,* the period of the *intellectual incarnations three shells,* and the period of the *supernormal incarnations two shells*; in fact there are 98 *instinctual* incarnations, 147 *intellectual* incarnations, and 98 *supernormal* incarnations, for a total of 343.

"Wait a minute!" Roberta said again to abate the fire in her mind, "Then there are always 343 human incarnations?"

"On an average, yes, but the human incarnations can be a few more or a few less, according to the evolutive capacity of the individual who manages to constitute his consciousness with a greater or lesser number of returns on the physical plane."

They were traveling along a Roman consular road lined by immense trees. Roberta could not accept that such difficult teaching could be useful, and said again: "What use is all this teaching?"

Julius smiled and opened his briefcase, taking out his agenda. "Here is an answer to your question given by the Guides during a large gathering, that of the NAF group in Rome," he said. "I still have the answer in my agenda, because I just finished transcribing it yesterday." He read:

Question: *Cui prodest* – to whose benefit is it – to know so many things?

Brother A: This is a valid question, which I shall answer on different levels. The first of these, I should point out, lies right in the openness and spiritual change enacted by the participants during these gatherings.

You see, just as the spirit is fed by harmony, and the heart is nourished by feelings, so is the mind nourished by logic and knowledge. Once again I tell you that no creature achieves evolution without passing through the satisfaction of all its components. If truly something changes inside you, it is because you have loved, understood, and felt this thing. The order in which you do these three activities is not important; there are those who feel, love, and reason. There are those who reason, feel, and love, and so on.

This, truly, seen from the standpoint of the final purpose, does not have major weight. The important thing is that one loves, thinks, and feels harmoniously, otherwise one would fall once again into the paradox of philosophies, which satisfy the mind but not the heart, or religions, that satisfy the heart and more rarely the spirit, but not the mind.

You must learn to grow in a homogeneous way because if you do not manage to make the parts of yourself agree with yourself then you will not succeed in making *your all* agree with others. Do you understand this?

The real physician is the one who does not treat the symptom but the origin of the illness by observing the symptom. It is the one who is not concerned solely with the body but also with the spirit of his patients, who does not neglect the psychological effects of pain, suffering and illness.

In the same way we, who try to be thaumaturgists, must not make the mistake of satisfying only a part of you, and, even though you may feel more one way than another, it is our duty to bring you, all of you, to feel in a homogeneous manner. We would do you harm if we only amazed you with the beauty of our eloquence or if we shackled you every time to the strictness of our reasoning or – even more – if we tried to dazzle you by taking you to a consciousness that had not gone through all the rest.

It is not our intention to harm you but to help you find your path towards evolution. This is why we use logic; it is not in order to put a chain on you. When we talk to you and arouse your emotions it is not to veil your eyes with feelings. On the contrary, we try to make logic break the chains of your preconceptions and make feeling reawaken your astral part, teaching you to feel emotion.

Therefore, whoever of you views the individual parts of this teaching as isolated or isolatable from the rest would fall into gross error. Every means we use works towards the growth of the relative part that is involved, and in a mediated way, also of the other parts.

So that you may not find yourselves one day – thinking back over this experience, or not being able to participate any more, or because the experience has come completely to an end, or because it has come to an end for you – so that you may not find yourselves, as I was saying, immersed only in a sterile memory of the emotions or an arid memory of the logic – confusing what is spiritual with what is produced by man. This is the reason why we teach you to love, to understand, to feel.

May peace be with you.

"What do you think?" Julius asked, closing his agenda.

"I think that if it is true that mediumship exists, it could be the science of sciences," Roberta answered. Then she added "I, however, am still on **Chekhov**'s side, when he said in his Notebook: 'When you're thirsty and it seems that you could drink the entire ocean that's faith; when you start to drink and finish only a glass or two that's science'."

"The Guides would add another parameter", Julius said, "that of *feeling*, which has nothing to do with either faith or science, and is our *essence*. To make us understand better what *feeling* is, the Guides use the metaphor of the eye. They explain that we see everything that surrounds us through the eye, but paradoxically the eye does not see itself. Well, this is it: the seat of feeling, the consciousness, is in the same position as the eye; feeling is manifested through the entire apparatus of reception and of presentation of ourselves in the world, but precisely for this reason, *feeling does not see itself,* because its function is so connatural with its being – there is no distinction between being, feeling and the function of feeling, but it is all one whole – that it is not possible to examine feeling if not in action. And in this action we do not examine *feeling* but the *effects of feeling*."

Therefore, for the Guides it is not possible to examine feeling under a microscope, since *feeling* is precisely the being-function apparatus that enables life in the world and the consequent evolution. We, instead, must ask ourselves questions about how our action presents itself to the world, and through these questions we shall be able to understand what conformation our *feeling* takes. Thus we should not seek to increase feeling, because if the eye is unhealthy and needs glasses, which are something external to it, in the same way it is not possible to act directly on feeling, but it is necessary *to operate via actions that are external to feeling* and that work to modify it."

The highway broadened into three lanes at that point and Roberta pulled into the centre lane. Here they were immediately overtaken, one could even say overcome, by a horde of motorcycles racing each other at high speed.

"How many illiterates in the art of feeling must there be among those madmen?" Roberta commented.

Julius did not answer, and Roberta asked "Is your silence meant to tell me that my feeling is inadequate?"

"In this case, what, in your opinion, would be an action *external to your feeling* that aimed at modifying it?" Julius asked.

"Maybe I should not have said that those bikers were feeling-illiterates?" Roberta guessed.

"Not only should you not have said it, but an *action external to feeling* is also not thinking what you thought when those people passed us," Julius said.

"Because I would have been wrong?"

"Because every judgment about others is illusory. Passing judgment creates friction with the Law, and friction in turn provokes correction by the Law."

"Your Guides often speak of *correction*", Roberta said, "and yet **Molière** in *The Misanthrope* says: 'Of all follies there is none greater than wanting to make the world a better place.' What would your Guides say about this statement?"

"That each person makes the world a better place by making himself a better person; this is how the Law corrects the world. But I doubt that Molière believed in self-correction."

"Because Molière did not understand life?" Roberta was taken aback.

"Who really understands life? Does an intellectual or an artist, for the very fact that they are such, maybe understand life?"

"So then, who?"

"The true mystic, for example, understands life, because at certain moments he lives to feel and only feeling understands life."

"What moments?"

"Those when the mystic transcends himself as a man and discovers himself to be *superman*, the moments when he moves his awareness on to the plane of consciousness and experiences the fusion with the Absolute-All-One, which is the ultimate reality."

"Maybe I understand," Roberta said. "It is the moments when the mystic finds again in consciousness what he had earlier understood only with the mind."

Meanwhile they had reached the little town where the company they were calling on was located, so Julius did not have time to answer. They drove down the crowded narrow streets and soon arrived in front of their prospective customer's establishment. On the front wall of the building, someone had written in red paint: "When justice comes, you will spit blood."

"A good start to our negotiations!" Julius commented as he got out of the car.

"Perhaps the person who wrote that did not know this one by **Ataturk**: 'The sword of Justice sometimes strikes the innocent, but the sword of History always strikes the weak'."

"Perhaps the Guides would say that Ataturk did not know either what Justice was or what History was," Julius said. "Otherwise he would not have said that Justice can strike the innocent. The Law never allows someone to suffer unjustly; for the Law, no one is ever weak by chance either in history or in daily life, because if one is weak, his weakness has to teach him something he has not understood."

"It seems to me that your Guides call *collective karma* the experience by which a people is weak and is subjected to the force of other peoples," Roberta said. "Is this true?"

"Precisely," Julius said proudly.

They went into the building and asked for the owner. Then they walked across huge open spaces and came to an office, where they were greeted by an elderly man who demonstrated great vitality.

"I asked you to come", the man said straight off, "because I have a lot of employees and I have decided to see to the cleaning of their work clothes and the cafeteria linens in house."

"That's our job," said Roberta.

"It's not only your job, but your attitude towards service that makes you appear open and willing to help a possible customer," the man said. "I too have always served others first, and then the company, and during the war I even built the house of God."

"Really?" said Roberta, to soften the tone of their meeting.

"That's right," said the company owner. "During World War II I was fighting in North Africa and was taken prisoner by the English, who sent me with another thousand prisoners to a POW camp. In the beginning the camp consisted of thirteen barracks, but we build concrete sidewalks and planted flowers, so that the whole area was transformed. We also created a little square, where the English allowed us to raise a statue of Saint George, which I made of a framework of barbed wire covered with concrete. We even built a little theatre with a stage and a recreation hut, which had with a pool table. But one thing was still missing: a chapel. We Italian prisoners sent a request to the inspector of the POW camps…"

"Imprisonment is a forceful experience", Julius commented, "because it gives you time and space to know yourself."

"That I know!" the man cut him off, and continued. "Towards the end of 1943 the English adapted two Nissen huts for the prisoners and I thought of using one as a school and the other as a church. Then, with the commander's permission, I started working on a chapel at the farthest end of the camp. While I worked, many ideas took shape in my head, but each one had to be carried out with the simplest materials, like scraps, salvage, and improvised means."

"In fact, the will can materialize the desire on the physical plane," Julius said. "The more the will, which is vibration of *mental matter*, is sustained, the greater probability it has to mould the desire, which is vibration of *astral matter*, on the physical plane.

"I did not mean that," the man said sharply, and went on, "With my fellow prisoners I formed a team of helpers and began working. The apse, which was the original concept, required a great deal of time and work. We covered the corrugated metal of the hut with plaster; the altar, altar rail, and holy water font, all designed by me, were modelled out of concrete. Behind the altar, up to the ceiling, between two stained-glass windows depicting Saint Francis of Assisi and Saint Catherine of Siena, we painted the Virgin and Child, which I copied from a prayer card I carried with me during the war."

"The image is not important," Julius said. "What is important is how much you believe in it…"

Not even this time did the man stop talking. "For the doors at each end of the chapel, we bought a length of gold-coloured damask, paid for with money from the prisoners' charity fund. Then we made two iron candlesticks and four brass ones. We took the wood for the tabernacle from a wrecked ship. I frescoed the ceiling with symbols of the four evangelists, and on the walls below, on either side of the chapel, I painted two cherubim and two seraphim…"

"The cherubim and seraphim are *higher sovereign spirits*," Julius said. "The Spirit Unit uses these groups of entities, which our religion calls *choirs*, to manifest itself; these are immensely evolved entities. They are a sublime, marvellous *machinery* of nature, which takes care of the functioning of the Cosmos."

Visibly annoyed, the old man continued, "In the centre of the vault I put the white dove symbolizing the Holy Spirit."

"Do you know who the Holy Spirit is?" Julius interrupted him again.

"No!" the man exclaimed.

"The Holy Spirit of whom Christ speaks is mediumship, in other words the Consciousness that speaks to mankind more and more through individuals called mediums."

The man remained impassive.

Once again Julius agreed with the Guides that there is nobody more crystallized than the fideist, who does not have faith but an obtuse faithfulness. Nonetheless he tried to set forth the truths in which he believed, while the company owner imposed those of his religious organization.

The man blustered on "There was such a blaring contrast between the apse as it was finished and the rest of the chapel that one of the prisoners, Lacanna, a skilled ironworker who before the war had studied his trade in America, was moved to make a wrought iron screen dividing the space, once again to my design. The work took four months and the screen is still one of the chapel's main glories."

"In reality the chapel has become a monument because it was made by prisoners and not because of its actual artistic qualities," Julius said at this point.

"What?" reacted the businessman who was supposed to be buying dry-cleaning machines.

"I mean that thousands of people have done maybe even the same things, and yet no trace has remained of them anywhere, because they were not prisoners. A *vibratory* event, an experience, in and of itself has no objective value, if not for the way in which it is *felt* by those who live it."

"Have you ever been back to your chapel?" Roberta asked to break the tension created by Julius's words.

"In 1960", the man resumed, visibly annoyed, "thanks to a generous grant from the BBC, I was invited for three weeks by the chapel's preservation committee. During my stay, with the aid of a local painter, I restored the paintings on the interior and made numerous repairs to the exterior. I remember that during the Mass commemorating the restoration of the chapel, I was the first to receive Holy Communion…."

"What does *communion* mean to you?" Julius asked.

"It is an obligation," the man answered.

"Which is?"

"An act that religion tells me to do and I do."

"Fool!" Julius erupted. "You deserve for us to stop feeding your ego and go away. All this work during and after the war, you did in the most complete state of thoughtlessness. The *communion* of which you speak is the intimate harmony of beings, the All-One, which is the key to understanding the importance in the teachings of Christ and the Bible of the communion of beings, their intimate union, their spiritual copulation in One Sole Being, which at the same time is the sum and the transcendence of All!"

At this point the elderly businessman stood up and dismissed the two sales representatives without even shaking their hands. When they were outside the building, Roberta looked at Julius resignedly, as though to tell him that if he had more patience, maybe they would have sold four industrial-size machines. Julius vigorously retorted that, if they had created-perceived this episode, then it had to be experienced both by them and by the businessman. He added that he had to learn from the episode to be more tolerant, while the elderly businessman could understand that he possessed an ego that was still very robust. Then Roberta quoted this line – "People understand me so little that they do not even understand when I complain of being misunderstood."

"To whom are you referring?" Julius asked when they were back in the car.

"To you, but the line is **Kierkegaard**'s," Roberta said. "What would the Guides say about the lack of understanding that just happened between you and the businessman?"

"Surely they would say that I could have avoided that lack of understanding, listening patiently to the man's story and letting his ego take over our meeting, which by the way was supposed to be a business meeting," Julius said. "But since nothing happens by chance, I repeat that not even my lack of tolerance was useless, and even if it will not fail to have an effect on me, it might also become a reason for reflection for the businessman. At bottom, even the lack of understanding of which Kierkegaard speaks is an opportunity for evolution on the part of the *misunderstood*."

"Certainly, that old man was hard-headed," Roberta commented. "He threw us out without standing on ceremony as soon as he was sure that you did not bend to his interests. Maybe **Mencius** is right when he says: 'Never has a man who has bent himself been able to make others straight'."

"In fact, the Guides would say that the man who has truly bent himself, that is to say 'is strong with himself', knows that he has achieved that strength through his experiences and thus will never seek *to make others straigh*t, because he respects others' weakness and knows that each one can only go beyond himself on his own."

"Relieve my curiosity," Roberta said. "Would you be able to do without the Guides?"

"The Guides, yes; the reason they manifest themselves, that is to say, their teaching, no."

They came to a red light and stopped in front of the pedestrian crossing. In front of them a group of people crossed the street, and right when the 'Walk' sign started blinking, a young man hurried through the crosswalk with feminine movements, swaying as though on a catwalk. He eyed the drivers waiting for the green light. Maybe he was gay. Someone yelled at him, racing his motor. Roberta drove through the light and then pulled over to the side of the road. She opened her agenda and read a thought she had taken from **Kenko**'s *Essays on Idleness:* "However gifted and accomplished a young man may be, if he has no fondness for women, one has a feeling of something lacking, as of a precious wine cup without a bottom."

"For Kenko, that gay boy would not have a chance," Roberta commented.

"For Kenko maybe not, but for the Guides he would", Julius said, "because for them homosexuality is nothing more than a stratagem by nature for limiting births."

"Do you mean homosexuality is not an anomaly?" Roberta asked.

"According to human logic it is, but according to the logic of the Law it is not," Julius said. "When mankind becomes too numerous, we have many cases of sexual inversion, which are a means by which the Law brings the complex of incarnations into balance. In fact, homosexuals do not have children. Another matter is homosexuality observed from below, that is to say from our relative way of seeing, by which whoever experiences the 'vibratory event called homosexuality' in an earlier incarnation did not want children or aborted or misused his masculinity or persecuted homosexuality; all these are contributing causes that bring about sexual inversion."

"Then your Guides would not agree with **Saint Bernardino of Siena** either, when he thundered in his *Prediche Volgari:* 'To the devil's house, to the devil's house you go, O Sodomite!' would they?"

"How could they? If the Guides don't accept either the real existence of the devil or the unworthiness of the homosexual experience!"

"Your Guides don't even accept the existence of the devil?" Roberta exclaimed wonderingly.

"They admit the existence of the devil's *thought form* but not the existence of the devil."

"What is the difference?"

"A chasm of difference, because all the appearances of the devil, real or presumed, that have been perceived by witches or even by persons who have been proclaimed saints by our religion, have never demonstrated an actual existence of the devil, but only the existence of a *thought form*, in other words an *ideational container,* fed by all those who over the centuries have believed in the devil. It is no coincidence, now that fewer and fewer people adhere to the Catholic tradition, that those who still see the devil have practically died out."

"And the smell of sulphur, the goat horns and hooves that people who have seen the devil always talk about?"

"That's exactly it: the tradition has always spread the idea of the devil with these characteristics, which the *thought form of the devil* has fed on over the centuries. If everybody who believed in the devil during these centuries had imagined him with different characteristics, the *thought form* of the devil would have contained other information, and consequently, the *thought form* would have manifested itself differently to the *sensitives* who entered into contact with it, in other words it would have *freed* other information."

"Can you give me an example?" Roberta said.

"If, for example, the organization that calls itself 'Rome Sports Association', the official name of the soccer team followed by hundreds of thousands of enthusiastic fans, had originated two-thousand years ago, with its same symbol of the she-wolf nursing Romulus and Remus, now some sensitive would enter into contact with the *thought form of the Rome Sports Association*, which would *free the visual information* which the fans would have believed over the course of two-thousand years. And one of these could be the she-wolf nursing the twins."

Roberta inevitably asked "Then not even **Nabokov** was right when he said: 'Solitude is the playing field of Satan'."

"Precisely. Nabokov was right for those who believe in the *thought form of Satan*", Julius said, "but the fact remains that Satan does not exist. Therefore, for the Guides, solitude can be the playing field of the *thought form of Satan* but certainly not of Satan."

They were traveling along the main road of Torre Spaccata, where urban decay prevailed everywhere. Groups of young people were hanging out in front of the coffee shops, oily with black grease and passion, and yet many people were smiling, as though they were happy with that life.

Roberta commented "In slums like this I understand **Li Li Weng**, when in *How to be Happy, though Poor* he said: 'The art of being happy even though poor can be summed up in just one phrase: it could be worse'."

"I do not believe those kids are happy", Julius said, "and I do not believe either that being happy is a skill. I believe instead that it is a nature which a being achieves through evolution and certainly not when he is still a man. I do not believe either that a poor man can be happy saying 'it could be worse'. On the contrary, I believe, as we have seen, that even a poor man can access a state of consciousness that the Guides call *satisfaction*. This is the *feeling* that, for whoever is still human, comes closest to happiness as we understand it."

Suddenly a luxurious Mercedes with darkened windows passed them like a mysterious vision and squeezed them against the parked cars lining the road. Roberta grabbed the wheel as though to follow the Mercedes. Then she limited herself to cursing in her own way, exclaiming, "**Mao Tse-tung** was right when he said that in a society divided into classes, every person lives as a member of a given class, and there is no thought that does not bear the imprint of a class."

"There is no thought, nor way of passing!" Julius smiled, "even if the Guides explain that social classes will disappear..."

"I don't think so", Roberta said, "because we are still divided into interest groups and thus into classes."

"This is the way it seems to you, because the *group I*, which is the social class, disguises itself constantly," Julius said. "But, at the end of the Age in which we are now living – the Age of the Son or of Love – in the next-to-last Age, which will begin in 2410, the social classes will be definitively gone. Then the Age of the Holy Spirit or of Wisdom will begin, during which more and more people will discover living in consciousness, which is true life."

"I believe instead that the social classes will always exist," Roberta insisted. "Just think of who has money and who doesn't!"

"But note: the social class is the place where the *group I* aggregates", Julius said, "but since evolution leads to the consumption of the *individual I* that makes up the *group I*, the social classes will die out more and more, even if this will take a long time..."

"On the subject of class", Roberta said, "what do you think of this saying? 'The thief and the duke are the same person'."

"Who said that?" Julius asked.

"**Chuang Tzu**. It is in the *Sacred Book of Nan Hua*."

"Another Eastern sage. Why are you now quoting Orientals so much?" Julius asked.

"Because it seems to me that they have many affinities with the philosophy of your Guides."

"In effect, that is so: for the Guides the East is more evolved than the West. This is true naturally for the average of the incarnate beings in those places. And too, by evolution the Guides mean spiritual advancement and certainly not technological civilization."

"So the United States, for example, would be less evolved than India, where thousands of people are still dying of hunger?" Roberta asked sceptically.

"We have talked about that. The living conditions which in India are often disastrous do not invalidate the *middle level of evolution* of that community of incarnate beings, which remains higher than that of so-called rich countries."

Roberta was still doubtful.

"Getting back to Chuang Tzu", Julius picked up the thread again, 'the thief and the duke' expresses well the absolute relativity that prevails in the *planes of perception*, which are the physical, astral and mental planes, a relativity that is the reflection of the *I-not-I duality*. But for the law of evolution, relativity does not exist; what exists is the *vibratory cipher* of the experience, not the *title* of the experience.

This means that the Law does not care if someone who steals a piece of wood is called a thief and one who steals a kingdom is called a duke. It only cares about the *evolutive essence*, the *vibratory coefficient* which the experience of stealing has imparted to the so-called thief and the so-called duke."

"Then we cannot ever be sure of anything!" Roberta protested. "According to your Guides a 'Great' who possesses the truth does not exist!"

"He or she does not exist, because the truth is possessed only by the person who, paradoxically, is no longer a person. Only then does the individual *know* the truth, because he *is it*."

"I'll bet that for your Guides not even **Aristotle** is right, when in the *Metaphysics* he says: 'We do not know the truth if we do not know the cause'."

"Certainly, because even knowing the cause, we cannot know the truth. To know the truth one has to *be it* and when *one is truth – one is also the cause*, but here we get back to the point: in order to *be a truth* one cannot be a *human being* because humans, with the *mind*, can only *know*, never *be*. And one can *be a truth* only when he has *so broadened his consciousness as to encompass that truth in it*. And when does he achieve this consciousness? When we no longer live by the mind, but by consciousness, that is to say, *we are no longer human beings*."

"You mean that, if we are still human beings, we are never a truth?" Roberta asked.

"We are limited truths. The love for our children, for example, love that *we do not know but are*, gives a very vague idea of what the Guides mean by *being a truth*."

"Then what would your Guides say about the poet **Gibran**, who in *The Prophet* gives a relative meaning even to love for one's children?"

Roberta opened her agenda and read:

Your children are not your children.
They are the sons and daughters of Life's longing
for itself.
They come through you but not from you,
And though they are with you, yet they belong not to you.

You may give them your love but not your thoughts.
For they have their own thoughts.
You may house their bodies but not their souls,
For their souls dwell in the house of tomorrow, which
you cannot visit, not even in your dreams.

"In fact, Gibran refers to states of consciousness much higher than those in which one loves one's children", Julius said, "because even the love for one's children is a *truth that is a point of passage.*"

"Why – does one love from a minimum to a maximum?" Roberta asked.

"Certainly. The individual approaches Love, which is its evolutive goal, beginning by loving from a minimum, that is, only itself, to a maximum, which is love for the All, in order to arrive at Love with a capital L through countless states of consciousness. These are love for another individual – which is already something different from oneself, and is provoked by the sexual instinct – love for one's children, which are always flesh of one's flesh, and so on and so forth."

"Therefore, does one love in concentric circles?" Roberta asked.

"All of feeling proceeds by concentric circles; the widest feeling always contains the less wide. Evolution always proceeds like this."

Roberta opened her agenda again. "There are, however, those who say that evolution does not exist," she said. "**Picasso**, for example, in the *Conversation* with Marius de Zoyas stated: 'I was surprised by the use and abuse that is made of the word evolution. I do not evolve, I am. In art there is neither past nor future. Art that is not in the present will never be'."

"Perhaps Picasso says this because evolution is not created but discovered," Julius said. "From this perspective Picasso is right, but he is wrong when he says 'I do not evolve', because evolution *reveals itself in the eternal present.* Thus not only will art *that is not in the present never be,* but everything that is not in the present does not exist."

Roberta was quiet a long time. She was trying in vain to reconcile the thought of great men with the thought of the Guides.

After a while Julius asked her "Have you suddenly discovered yourself to be a student of silence?"

"No, it is just that what the Greats say almost never fits with what your Guides say," Roberta said. "It is as though each referred to a different logic."

"It could not be any other way, because the 'Greats', no matter how great they are, were and are incarnate beings. In other words, they are tied to the human condition, to the cycle of rebirths, while the Guides have definitively left behind the *evolutive environment called Earth* and no longer access a human logic..."

"Speaking of being a *student of silence,* what is your opinion of this line that **Pascal** writes in his *Pensées*: 'The eternal silence of these infinite spaces terrifies me'."

"Exactly. For Pascal, who was still a man, the silence of infinite spaces existed because space still existed. For the Guides, on the other hand, who have definitively transcended the physical plane and with it time and space, the silence inspired by space does not exist."

They had reached the wall around their factory and parked in front of the offices, which sat dwarfed by two enormous warehouses on either side. Roberta and Julius were tired and disappointed by the call that had not gone well. They got out of the car and saw on the wall in front of them a graffiti someone had left during the night: "Only God is."

"That's the same phrase we see written on the highway overpasses," said Roberta.

"It's a shame that the same line is not written everywhere," Julius commented. "It sums up very well the state of mind of ordinary people, who do not understand God but they feel him. For that matter, even an atheist reaches the point of feeling him."

"In fact", Roberta agreed, "**Gandhi** says that God is moral consciousness. He is even the atheism of the atheist."

"That is wonderfully the case," Julius said. "God is a state of consciousness and as such there are also those who do not believe in his existence, because the relationship between God and man cannot be compressed into a religion, but is intimate, total, and belongs to all."

"Then **Mohammed** is right too, when he says, 'There is no other God than Allah'."

"Yes, of course. This phrase is the equivalent of the Judaeo-Christian commandment 'You shall have no other gods before me.' Allah is not one particular god, like Jupiter in mythology, but is the Absolute. The Guides manifest themselves now in a diffused way to announce that it is time to leave behind the figurative images of the religions, which are fine for people who are still spiritual children – otherwise intelligence will remain solely the province of materialists. It is time to understand that material and spiritual reality is one sole thing and that one can also draw near to this one reality outside religions.

The time is over when the truth of the spirit belonged to the fairy-tale world of the dogmas. A new way of living is about to rise, that of consciousness, and man is about to emerge from the confused world of spiritual childhood to enter that of adulthood. This is why the Guides proclaim the dawn of a new Age, the Age of Consciousness."

ABOUT THE AUTHOR

Vitaliano Bilotta

Vitaliano Bilotta has been a teacher, journalist and trade unionist in a union inside Public Education. He has studied the philosophy of reincarnation and its dissemination for over forty years, applying it to life through the narrative form. He is passionate about the hypothesis of reincarnation, attending large mediumship gatherings that provide all-encompassing teachings of Reality.

Comments and teachings contained in his books are from syncretic study that the author has drawn from sources of wisdom, which are listed here, according to the chronology in which they were studied:

Allan Kardec - Cerchio Firenze 77 - Cerchio Ifior - Pietro Ubaldi - Cerchio Esseno - Cerchio Chesed - Cerchio Marina - Marcello Creti - Cerchio medianico Kappa - Demofilo Fidani - Punto F - Soggetto - Onda G - Cerchio d'oro - La voce interiore - Umanità e movimento - Altre fonti italiane e straniere. (Cerchio translates as Circle)

As an author he has books with various publishers

Edizioni Einaudi:
- *Fui chiamato dal presidente (I Was Called by the President)* under pseudonym of Antonio Caselle. Preface by Natalia Ginzburg.

Edizioni Mediterranee:
- *Il dizionario del Cerchio Firenze 77 (The Dictionary of the Florence 77 Circle)*
- *Essere e divenire (Being and Becoming)*
- *Cerchio medianico Kappa: Verso la Scintilla (Towards the Spark)*
- *Il nuovo libro degli spiriti (The new book of spirits)*

Interactive narrative:
- *La vera realtà. (The True Reality.)*
- *Perché la vita è così. (Because life is like that.)*

Il contatto con i piani superiori di esistenza: (The contact with higher planes of existence)
- *Iniziazione al channelling. (Initiation to channelling)*

The posthumous books of Amedeo Rotondi:
- *Le leggi del pensiero (The Laws of Thought)*
- *Le grandi profezie sul futuro dell'umanità (The Great Prophecies about the future of humanity)*
- *La potenza creatrice del pensiero (The Creative Power of Thought)*
- *Pensieri per una vita serena (Thoughts for a peaceful life)*

Edizioni Hermes:
Interactive narrative:
- *La fattura d'amore. (The Spell of Love)*

Allan Kardec section:
- *Dopo Allan Kardec (After Allan Kardec with audio CD that documents the activities of **Evolvenza**).*

Rumanian publisher **Nemira:**
- *Initiere in channelling. (Initiation in channelling)*

I Libri del Casato:
Interactive narrative:
- *Il mistico di città. (The City Mystic)*
- *Il pensiero dei Grandi commentato alla luce dell'insegnamento dei Maestri (Thoughts of the Greats, commented on in the light of the teaching of the Masters)*
- *La reincarnazione spiegata ai ragazzi (Reincarnation explained to children)*
- *Fui chiamato dal presidente (I was called by the President)*
- *La forma pensiero (The Thought Form)*
- *Omaggio ad Allan Kardec (Tribute to Allan Kardec)*

For the WEB:
Evolvenza Vitaliano Bilotta.   www.evolvenza.it

He also writes for the Italian monthly magazine *Giornale dei misteri (Journal of the mysteries)*

Lightning Source UK Ltd.
Milton Keynes UK
UKOW01f0820041015

259804UK00001B/8/P

9 781908 421142